GRACIOUS
— and —
STRONG

How to Rise Above the
Unexpected Left Turns
of Life and Leadership

CELIA SWANSON
with Tammy Kling

Clovercroft Publishing

Gracious and Strong: How to Rise Above the Unexpected Left Turns of Life and Leadership

©2018 by Celia Swanson

Published by Carpenter's Son Publishing, Franklin, Tennessee

Published in association with Larry Carpenter of Christian Book Services, LLC
www.christianbookservices.com

Edited by Tammy Kling and Tiarra Tompkins

Cover Design by Sarah Thurstenson

Interior Design by Adept Content Solutions

Printed in the United States of America

ISBN   Hardcover   978-1-945507-76-2
            Paperback   978-1-945507-82-3

OnFire Books
Helping world changers share their story

CONTENTS

GRATITUDE

In gratitude...

To all my mentors, sponsors and leaders who chose to invest in my leadership journey and career growth. Your lessons fell on fertile soil.

To all the team members who chose to follow me and define me as a leader. You held me accountable to live up to your highest expectations.

To all my mentees who allowed me to invest in you during our many development experiences. I received so much more from you as a result of our time together.

To Kyndall who keeps me grounded in life. You are a remarkable person and I am extremely proud of you! The role that brings me the greatest joy is being your Mom.

Thank you for grooming me to be a Gracious and Strong leader.

INTRODUCTION

Where are you on your leadership journey?

Every one of you is on a different path.

You may be on the fast track, focused and achieving extraordinary growth in your career.

Or you may have bigger dreams and higher hopes, wrestling with the tension of who you are versus who others expect you to be. You have probably come a long way in your career, and you are moving quickly, but perhaps you are unsure how you feel about your next steps or your ambition and drive. Now is the time to evaluate and take stock of where you are. Welcome to a safe place to do it, absent of bosses, leadership evaluation, or criticism. Welcome to a place where you can self-evaluate, learn, and assess your next steps.

No matter where you are in your career or life, my prayer is that you'll take home something valuable. It doesn't matter if you're on top of the world feeling strong and empowered, or feeling defeated and frustrated. Every one of you experiences wins and losses on this journey called life. I'll share mine with you, and I'll ask poignant questions designed to make you think. Ultimately it's about designing your own life. It's about becoming the very best leader you can be.

What does leadership mean to you?

This book will help you navigate these important questions and face your fears in order to understand your true life calling and purpose. Throughout my leadership journey, I've discovered that my own calling is centered on developing women and preparing them to take thoughtful risks. I want to empower women to thrive in whatever they do, whether it's as a mother, a wife, or in a business leadership position. It took years for me to see myself this way and a lot of failures and victories.

But let's not overlook the men. Men are such an important part of who I have become and have been some of my biggest supporters and mentors along the way. If you're a woman and you believe that men don't want you to get ahead, I encourage you to rethink that as you read through this book. Reach out to the strong men in your life for leadership advice. You won't regret it!

After decades in corporate America, I understand the struggles of women at a very real and personal level. I've reaped great rewards from my career and spent a lot of time learning the "hard-won" lessons of breaking the glass ceiling at the world's largest company and in many board rooms. One of my greatest professional achievements was becoming the first female executive vice president at Walmart Inc. and blazing trails for other women, (and men, too) along the way.

But for years, I wrestled with the tension of who I am versus who others expected me to be. I lived in conflict, trying to blend those expectations. I lost sleep over being good enough, and I overcame significant business and personal challenges, just like you.

I reached a point where my husband and I had to decide which career we would ultimately chase—and finally we decided it would be mine. That later resulted in his decision to be a stay-at-home dad to our daughter at a time when it was not popular for men to make that choice!

He was always supportive, and we approached everything as a team.

Then, at the peak of my career, I lost my husband to a sudden, fatal heart attack.

Even now, this is difficult to write. When I look back on those dark years, I can barely believe I've gotten through them, but I did, one step at a time. I realized that I'm not in control of a lot of things. I realized that, as much as we had planned for the best possible option, we had no control over the outcome and that life would ultimately throw us curve balls.

How you handle those curve balls is integral to your success in life. Don't fear them, but don't think they'll never come, either. How you manage the adversity is the truest test of what being a leader really is.

Leadership means different things to different people. What does it mean to you?

Under the leadership of Lee Scott, I was promoted to the position of executive vice president at Walmart Inc. While Lee was CEO, Walmart Inc. grew to be in the number one spot on the Fortune 500 list. We had the largest volume of any company in the world. But being the biggest was never our goal. Our mission was to be the best. Lee was named one of *Time* magazine's most influential people in the world—not because of his position but because of his impact.

Positional leadership is temporary and doesn't define you as a great leader. Lee Scott was a transformational leader in many ways. He certainly saw the vision for creating a diverse, inclusive leadership team. At some times in your life, you'll have leaders like that; at other times, you'll have leaders who are less than memorable.

I served on Lee's executive committee for four years. I had been running a large division at Sam's Club for four years, and I drove a significant part of the Sam's Club division profit. My role was SVP, Marketing and Membership for the club division of Walmart Inc. And my P&L (profit and loss) increases were quite strong that year. I worked hard for this big promotion, shifting from a specialization career track in Human Resources to leading a broadening role running a large P&L. When Lee promoted me to EVP, I was the only woman on his executive committee for two years. Then he added three more women, knowing that three or more women would significantly shape the conversations, decisions, and results for Walmart Inc.

Lee was a visionary leader who saw the need for diversity in the senior leadership ranks. Women made 78 percent of the purchasing decisions at that time. He understood the importance of having women on the senior leadership team, and I was honored to be selected. I carried a huge responsibility on my shoulders, and I never forgot that. Throughout my years there, I continued to learn and grow, sharing my voice and representing so much more than just me. And my leadership style evolved.

Even after I acquired a big promotion like that, the title of EVP didn't automatically make me a leader. Leadership is not a title. Leadership is an honor and a responsibility bestowed by followers. Leadership is a relationship between those who aspire to lead and those who desire to follow.

Followership defines leadership. Servant leadership starts with a vision and ends with a servant's heart.

In my opinion, a true leader must be committed to lifelong learning, breaking through limiting beliefs, and making positive change—only in the organizations they work for but starting first within themselves.

I wasn't born a leader, but I learned how to be one.

When I first started out in the retail business working for a department store, I did not begin with a leadership title. Promotions followed quickly on the basis of my results, my behavior and my willingness to work hard. I had a passion for the customer and for seeing individuals and teams succeed. I was willing to step forward and do the extra work. Leadership is all about people, and I have always had a heart for people.

It took me a few years, in my early career journey, to realize that the executive leadership team didn't want me to be just like the men that were sitting in the boardroom. It became apparent that they actually wanted me to be authentically me! I brought a feminine perspective, and they welcomed it. I felt a responsibility to find and share my voice, and when I did, more doors started to open for me, and I was able to build my influence and impact. Maybe it was because I was bringing in a new point of view and sharing those ideas in a way that my point of view would be heard.

My role was to challenge the paradigms and represent the perspective of the majority of our customers and associates, not as person who was antagonistic but as a person who shared a different perspective in a conversation—one the men in that room could not have otherwise.

Being authentic has been a critical component to my leadership success. Otherwise, I would not be seen as real, sound real, or act real. You can't be concerned with making a mistake, and you can't be fearful about speaking up. It took me a long time to define myself and evolve into my own authentic brand of leadership.

When the realization that I needed to be authentic hit me, I began busting through those previous belief windows I had held about what it meant to be a woman in leadership. I realized, *"It is okay to be me!"* Often I was the only woman in the boardroom. I'm a girlie girl, and I love being feminine, but you did not see that kind of presence in the boardroom, so, at first, I struggled to be myself, and I dressed masculine. I experienced being ignored, talked over, and invisible in the room at times. It was frustration that drove me to decide to show up and be myself, and it worked! *Show up as you are.*

This advice is important in many areas of life, from your business to your personal relationships. *Show up as you are.* Bring your unique energy to the room, and people will take notice. Being an imposter is hard to maintain.

You are responsible for how you show up, your authenticity, and the impact you make on others, while delivering exemplary results. This book is for all leaders who desire to live and lead with purpose and meaning. It is for all leaders who aspire for significance and to leave the world better because of their influence and service. It is for leaders who feel stuck in survival mode and are willing to face their fears and dreams.

The five things you will take away from this book are as follows:

1. Finding true significance in everything you do in work and in life.

2. Having confidence in who you are as a leader; becoming an authentic leader.

3. Becoming a more selfless leader who creates opportunity for those around them to succeed; becoming a servant leader.

4. Looking back and looking ahead on a purposeful well-lived life.

5. Setting a strong example for yourself, your children, and your family.

This book was written with the busy leader in mind. There is a takeaway section at the end of each chapter that lists two to three questions or points for your personal reflection and application. Each chapter can be read as a stand-alone, or the entire book can be read as a story that builds upon every lesson to compel each of us to action.

I always felt a sense of responsibility when I was the only woman in the room, and I knew I was representing so many more people than just me. This public responsibility motivated me to put things in place that were foundational for the development of women. I did not achieve corporate success on my own. I was compelled to bring other women along, and I was compelled to help men do the same. As you read through this book I hope you feel inspired.

Leadership doesn't have to be about bullying, intimidation, or even passive-aggressive silence. Leadership can be authentically defined by you as you travel your own journey.

Please join me in modeling leadership that can best be described as Gracious and Strong.

Celia

Chapter 1
AUTHENTIC LEADERSHIP

"If your actions inspire others to dream more, learn more, do more, and become more, you are a leader."

—John Quincy Adams

What's your leadership style?

Leadership can be confusing, just for the sheer number of definitions, books written about it, and theories on the subject. It seems as if everyone these days has a different definition of leadership, and there are literally thousands of books written on the subject.

Today we are facing a real leadership deficit in our world.

Consultants and leadership companies have many assessments and strategies to teach managers and their teams how to adopt a variety of leadership styles, from strategic to transformational and from autocratic to charismatic. There are leadership "colors," leadership personality types, leadership assessments, leadership coaching programs, roundtables, clubs, DVDs, and masterminds. No wonder there are so many schools of thought and books out there on leadership! The landscape can be overwhelming to navigate.

Ultimately the best answer is this:

No matter what type of leader you want to be, make your commitment to be a servant leader first. Meaning, if you want to be a charismatic leader, be charismatic. (If you want to be a direct, transformational, or silent leader that's okay, too.) But first, above all else, be a leader who strives to serve others.

What does leadership mean to you?

Life and leadership are a series of choices. It's your choice as to the kind of leader you decide to be. I've worked with every kind of leader, employee, and colleague you can imagine, whether it was in the executive office, or in our stores or clubs, at the executive and associate level. Throughout it all, I have determined ultimately that the very best leaders are servant leaders.

Servant leaders are givers. They want to serve their employees, as well as the organization as a whole, in order to see everyone else rise.

If you were raised by a servant leader, you may have already become one. But if you weren't, you can adopt this principle of serving others first as you go about the task of becoming a strong, respected, and trustworthy leader in your life and family.

"Putting others first is a sign of character, not compromise!" ~ Mary Jenson

Serving others is your greatest reward! When we place our focus on others rather than on exercising power and control, we become effective leaders that others choose to follow. Servant leaders model action and therefore are change agents in the world. They are self-aware and don't display arrogance and overconfidence that so often accompany positions of power.

In the pages to follow, I'll talk about how you can evolve to the heights of putting others first. It can be a challenge for successful people to think this way, especially when we are groomed to focus on results first. Results are critical; they are the price of entry. But the more you succeed, the more tempting it can be to fall into the trap of resting in that success. Never rest in success. Never settle to maintain. Never be enamored with your own "press."

Leaders are lifelong learners, and leaving a legacy requires evolving from success to significance!

That means it's important to commit yourself to reinventing yourself, your mission, and your ability to influence and create impact often. Don't make the mistake of resting in past performances. You have to stay in development mode, always improving and getting stronger. My goal is to help you face into the hard-right decisions of life and leadership.

After decades of leadership in the corporate arena, I experienced several victories, and also failures! There were difficult conversations to navigate, obstacles along the way, and also major successes. Something that I tell others: leadership involves a lot of building and preparation.

Failing to prepare is a choice.

You will fail when you don't invest the time in preparation. Similarly, prepare for the possibility that you might fail, and even if you do, this can vastly improve your performance when you try again. There were many times in my life where it was proven that preparation would have been the key to a more successful outcome. Two times in particular come to mind, and, both times, my failure to prepare almost demolished me. One of those times occurred at an analyst meeting when I was asked questions that I didn't prepare for. The men, my peers on stage, had to step up when I was visibly stumped and unable to answer the questions. I had the opportunity to demonstrate my knowledge and proficiency about the business, but I froze and gave away that very public opportunity.

The second example occurred at an executive committee retreat when the chairman of the board asked me a specific question about how my business compared to that of my competition. I did not know the answer! I was embarrassed, and I never recovered in his eyes, in the eyes of my peers, and, more important, in my own eyes. It was at that very moment that I knew that my personal commitment would be to never fail to know my business better than anyone else and to always come prepared.

When I first stepped into an executive leadership role, I realized how much more impactful I became when applying authenticity in my leadership. Simple as that, everything changed. I didn't have to be gruff or rough or act like a man. I was tough, direct, and fair. I was feminine and decisive, and I could even wear lipstick! I was a girlie girl and voiced valuable opinions. Why not? I could serve others, be open and honest, and be vulnerable, too.

I learned to share my voice in a way that I could sway votes, help make change, and even change the perception about myself. I wasn't someone who didn't deserve to be in the room. I wasn't just in the room because I was a woman. I was somebody who would be able to make change, drive improvements, and help the organization and others be more successful.

One example is a day when there were four women in the boardroom. Every year we would be presented with the benefits package for the next budget this year. This included options that would be made available in the next calendar year for our associates.

It was always a question about what was most needed, balanced with what we could afford. For this particular year, we were presented with options that included well-baby care. The Benefits Team presented the choices and opened them up for discussion.

Well-baby care was an important consideration for addition this year, and Lee Scott wanted to ensure that he heard every voice around the table before we voted. He made it a point to hear from every woman in the room. Because I had been serving on the executive committee the longest, Lee called on me first.

I had to find my courage to tell my story in a way that I uniquely owned and to be persuasive in why I felt we should adopt well-baby care. So I did just that. I told them my personal story. It was a defining moment that happened shortly after I joined Sam's Club. My husband had been encouraged by our pediatrician to get public assistance for school vaccinations for my daughter. Immunizations were not covered by our company health care plan, and we were not aware of that. My husband was embarrassed and insisted we could afford the vaccinations, so she was immunized by the doctor. But, in his mind, he had been humiliated and couldn't believe that immunizations weren't covered. Because of that incident, it took me weeks to convince him that we had made the right choice to join Walmart and move our family. I never wanted another family to go through the same experience! It was time that we introduced well-baby care; it would be an important benefit to continue to attract and retain families to our company. This was a talent decision, not just a benefits decision.

The next woman jumped on my story and added her own. She said, "I had the same experience with my spouse when he took our daughter in to get her shots before she started school."

The next two women jumped in with similar personal stories. The entire room listened intently, and the decision now had a meaning much more than just financial. Our personal stories were not ones experienced by others in the room. They were personal stories experienced by many of our associates and their families.

That year we adopted well-baby care, and it was a defining moment for me. It was a galvanizing moment for the women in that room, and it was a critical opportunity for our company to reflect the values it represented in their actions—to be a family values-based company.

What if Lee hadn't asked me what my thoughts were? What if I had been afraid to speak up? What if I had been so concerned about fitting in that I didn't use my voice? Would another woman have been courageous enough to speak up instead of me? I had taken too long to feel comfortable on the executive committee to speak up on my own. This was the moment that showed me that my voice was critical. Had Lee not asked the question and I let it pass, I wouldn't be the leader I have grown to be today. I would have learned the lesson differently. There is a breakthrough moment when you start becoming the person you are meant to be. When you discover that your voice has the power to influence important decisions being made.

As I said before, authentic leadership is about remaining steadfast to your values. You can't make decisions based on fear or insecurity or on a false image you're trying to portray.

Authentic leadership causes you to dig deep, be clear about your own values and beliefs, and be who you are versus who others want you to be. Don't sell yourself short. You owe it to yourself to be authentic and to speak your mind. Authenticity adds color to the world, just as adversity adds a well-needed contrast. Bring your whole self. Bring your perspective. Bring your courage, and then be the one who initiates change.

Authenticity

What is your unique value that you bring to your work team or family?

Spend time writing it down and running it by your partner, a mentor, or a close personal colleague. Their perspective is not one that you can have. Ask to gain their point of view. Then own it! Some people are so afraid to speak up that they end up giving away their power. They have no voice because they're afraid to be unpopular or that their idea will be rejected.

Have you ever been in a situation where you were afraid to speak up?

What were you afraid of? Would it have changed the situation, or did your silence leave the opportunity to speak up and drive change to someone else?

Techniques you can use to reveal authenticity

1. I was given wise advice by a close friend and business colleague, Coleman Peterson, to sit at the front of the room and to be prepared to ask a thought-provoking question in every meeting you attend. Practice this technique and you will be much more comfortable speaking up.

2. The other technique is to say what needs to be said by sharing it in a factual story that no one can dispute. You own the story, and the result is what you are trying to influence. But you can rarely influence anything if you are seen as an antagonist, with no foundation for your opinion. No one can argue when you ground your point of view inside a

personal experience. The next time you're afraid to speak up, take a deep breath, and speak up anyway. Don't let these moments pass. Leadership is an evolution, and every year you can be better than the one before.

Chapter 2
FALLING FORWARD

"You gain strength, courage, and confidence by every experience in which you really stop to look fear in the face. You must do the thing you think you cannot do."

—ELEANOR ROOSEVELT

When my husband, David, and I got married, I was a junior in college studying fashion merchandising, and he was in his final year of his master's degree at the College of Architecture. We made an agreement that whichever career took off first, we would follow that person's career. We graduated from college and were both earning the same annual salary.

Never did I think my career was the one that would soar! His profession and the amount of education required to be an architect seemed much more substantial and aspirational than a career in retailing. But that was not the case. My career moved us from Lincoln to Omaha, Nebraska; on to Des Moines, Iowa; then to Denver, Colorado; and on to Bentonville, Arkansas. And David lived up to his commitment, even when it meant that he had to start over in a firm or join a start-up firm.

There were two occasions when I did not think he would follow my career, but he always did. And always at the sacrifice of his own. When we moved to Bentonville, Arkansas, he took the most drastic step in our dual-income partnership—he stepped out of the workforce to become a stay-at-home dad with our eight-month-old daughter. That was in 1994, when there were very few stay-at-home dads. And they were a particular anomaly in this small, rural town in the South.

We had been married seventeen years when he came to me and said, "There must be more to life that we can experience. Let's have a child." Children were not part of our plan, so I was shocked when the discussion came up.

Needless to say, having a child didn't fit into my life goals at the time, but that was one of the earliest indications that there are many surprises that would come our way in life. One of the things I learned from that experience is that your plan isn't always the way life will unfold. I didn't think

I would ever become a parent, but God blessed us with a daughter and proved he had a plan that included becoming parents.

I am *so* grateful that David had the vision and courage to propel us into parenthood. Despite his career in architecture, he offered to be a stay-at-home dad to allow me the flexibility to travel and work at the intensity level required to grow my career quickly. It was a great decision, but not without challenges. The dynamic we had to manage for the rest of our marriage was a difficult one. He was doing the most important work—raising a healthy, respectful, independent, contributing young adult. I was slaying dragons at the world's largest retailer. The two jobs did not compare when it comes to impact. But society and the community did not give the level of respect or stature to the full-time caregiver, and that impacted his ego and self-esteem.

David was an exceptional dad. He was there when she was sick; he took her to school and picked her up every day; and he was there when she took dance, Taekwondo, gymnastics, and horseback riding lessons. He was the driver, the head of the parent-teacher organization, the one who volunteered at the school, and the one who was in the dressing room doing costume changes and putting a bun in her hair. He was often the only dad among all the moms and relied on the moms for support and guidance. And they relied on him for heavy lifting, construction, and design. In the community, he did not care for the name Mr. Celia Swanson. He needed to make his own community contributions, and he needed to have a spouse that showed up to support his big moments as he had done for mine.

David was always my biggest advocate, but I was not always his. I would describe our relationship as "Green Acres." He was from the country, and I was from the city. One of the most valuable lessons I learned is to lift up your partner and be their biggest advocate. Invest time and genuine interest in the passions of your partner because you never know when that last day will come. Put them first more often than you put them second or third. Never put a child or children in the middle. Unfortunately, I learned all of this the hard way, after I got the call that my precious husband had died.

An Unexpected Gift—A Dog

That was the day after Labor Day, the three-day weekend when David and Kyndall made the long trip to Nebraska to go visit his mom. Kyndall had insisted that they must drive to see Grandma because she was convinced Grandma would not make it to Christmas. She had the outcome right, just the wrong person.

It was a nine-hour drive each way. Kyndall was a sophomore in college and home for a long weekend. She convinced him on Sunday, after pleading with him to make the long trip. I stayed back to bond with the dog. I am not a dog person, so this was completely out of character. But the dog had been dumped at the stables and was recovering from parvo. Someone had to care for her.

They drove to Nebraska, took his mom out for dinner, stayed overnight, and drove home the next day. That was Labor Day, and the drive home took many more hours than expected. David was experiencing serious back pain and had to stop frequently to get out of the truck and walk, so he gave Kyndall the "this was our life" tour.

They stopped at the first apartment we lived in, the church where we were married, the University of Nebraska Student Union where we met, Love Library, Sheldon Art Gallery, and the College of Architecture buildings on

campus (all important buildings in our early married life).
They drove by our second apartment in Lincoln, Nebraska,
and then on to Omaha to see our first condominium, his
first office at HDR Architecture and Design firm, and
the home office for the department store where I got my
start in retailing. Then they tackled the long stretch home,
passing fields of corn, milo, sunflowers, and soybeans. When
they finally got home, we hopped in the truck and went
to dinner on the Bentonville Square. He was dealing with
waves of pain in his back, thinking it was a kidney infection.

On Tuesday morning, we woke up to start the work
and school week. I asked him how was he feeling. He said
a little bit better but not well. I told him that I *had* to lead
this meeting and that I wanted him to call the doctor and
make an appointment. I kissed him good-bye and told him
that I loved him and that I would call him after my meeting.
Kyndall had a hair appointment before she returned to
school in Kansas. She kissed him good-bye and drove off.

It was Kyndall who found him. She was only nineteen
years old. He was her favorite person in life. She rushed to
action by calling a close personal friend and 911. When the
police got there, she was performing CPR, but he was gone.
It was a heart attack that took his life instantly. He never
responded to any of the medicines or treatment. His heart
muscle was damaged and did not respond. He had been
experiencing a heart attack for many days, and the muscle
was too weak to recover.

In an instant, Kyndall lost her dad. In an instant, I lost
my husband of thirty-six years. In an instant, our lives were
changed forever, and we were completely unprepared. We
were falling so fast, gripped in profound grief, but we were
required to make decisions and move forward. I refuse to be
defined as a widow. I choose every day to have courage and
make the hard-right decisions to embrace life. I had to do

it for me, but, far more important, I had to be there for my daughter and do it for her.

That is why I titled this chapter "Falling Forward." We were in a fast and deep fall. We had a choice—to fall back and live in the grip of grief and sorrow, to fall down and to keep falling down because we could not deal with the pain, or to fall forward and to choose to take small, slow steps to move forward. We chose to fall forward, no matter how hard each right decision was. Unexpected left turns and hard-right decisions—the circumstances you don't expect—the hard-right decisions you must make to move forward.

Nothing about this journey has been easy, nothing has been clear, nothing has been as we had dreamed or planned. But every step is a choice, every choice made in deep sorrow and with the belief that this is all a part of God's plan.

My story is built on the concept of unexpected left turns. Left turns can be events, circumstances, relationships, or unexpected tragedy from your past. I break down the concept of unexpected left turns in a future chapter. But it is important to face into them and to recognize how they are having an impact on where you are today.

"Falling Forward" has been one of the most difficult challenges to take on. It has been hard work—every day, at unexpected moments, with every choice. It took professional help, friends willing to walk with me through the setbacks and victories, and my facing into the moments where I was falling back. Far too often, I see people who have gotten stuck in the falling-down stage. It shows up in their everyday conversations, it shows up in future relationships, and it shows up at work in inappropriate storytelling and a need for continued sympathy.

I am asking you to pause with me and ask yourself, "What is my most painful memory?" Then write it down.

Don't just give me a top-of-mind answer. This question requires you to dig deep into your past and truly find the most painful experience you have ever faced. Dig deep and then write it down.

Now let's explore:

How is it impacting you today?

Is it impacting the relationships you have now?

Is it impacting your relationships at work?

It takes constant, disciplined, hard work to make the decisions to fall forward. It starts with recognizing that you are making choices to keep falling down or being stuck in the grip of your pain. My prayer for you is to find your path to fall forward. There is so much you have yet to experience and great potential in you to be a world changer.

My journey has been overwhelmingly hard. My daughter's journey has been equally hard. And I would give my life to change that for her. You see, I was not the close parent. So we have had a long road to building an everlasting bond.

Keep the lines of communication open, in good times and in bad; don't let a day go by that you don't show your loved ones you care. You never know when it will be the last chance you can.

Breaking Your Fall

Being stuck in grief happens to many people. I had to consciously write down daily goals that would move me forward in a positive way. And I had to reinvent my life.

Are you stuck in the grips of fear, change, or grief?

Start your journey forward by identifying and envisioning success without grief. Call out to yourself what you are most afraid of. Start your journey forward by identifying and envisioning success without grief. Picture what your life will be like when you are no longer held back in the grips of grief. Find the positives that bring you joy. Envision your life when you successfully face into your current state.

Let others help you; reach out to professionals or trusted friends who you know have your best interests at heart. And then begin to dismantle your fear; understand it, but do not accept being stuck in it.

Practice gratitude. I thought that was a hokey suggestion and pure nonsense. But when I was at my lowest low, I decided to start my day with a reflection on gratitude. It changed my entire perspective. I had to practice the art of gratitude. And then I began to share my gratitude with those around me who mattered.

Instead of falling prey to self-survival mode—fall forward!

Step 1: Face into reality.

Step 2: Own what you should own.

Step 3: Make a hard-right decision to step back into life. Take small steps and rebuild your strength.

Step 4: Find joy and satisfaction.

This may sound like happy talk, but I challenge you to give it a try. You will be building a plan with steps and personal commitments at each stage.

I wrote my career plan when I was just getting started, and I pulled it out and held myself to the milestones I had set. But I had to write a new one when my life turned upside down. Build your plan to achieve joy, and then keep measuring your progress.

Chapter 3
FEARS AND LIMITING BELIEFS

"If you accept a limiting belief, then it will become a truth for you."

—Louise Hay

Everyone in life struggles with some form of fear, whether it's in business, as you're about to enter a room and deliver the biggest presentation of your life, or in your personal life. Ultimately, leaders have to learn how to address their fears each and every day. How will you slay your dragons? One by one, one day at a time, and often one step at a time as it happens. Part of being a servant leader is understanding that everyone is afraid.

It is not true that fears are "false events appearing real." Fears are actually real, and a leader helps others identify and walk through them.

One of the fears many of us have is the fear of not being good enough. I think this particularly applies to women. As I was gaining more responsibility and being given progressively larger roles, I often thought to myself, *When are they going to discover that I am not ready for this new role?* Every time I have a fear, it's a trigger to examine my belief windows.

Belief windows are a concept one of my early mentors, speaker Tony Jeary, taught me. Essentially, he said, "Everyone grows up and views the world through a certain lens or set of beliefs which inform how we think, feel, and apply to make our life decisions. Belief windows can be limiters, or they can be a catalyst to break through what may appear to be unattainable."

What do you believe about yourself and your life?

I've learned that there are many times when I've had incorrect beliefs that require me to break through them in order to think differently about how to succeed. This is absolutely true for all of us, and if you're self-aware, you can learn how to identify your limiting beliefs and broaden your perspective to discover what is possible. It's important to do a self-assessment routinely, not to be critical, but to assess and eliminate the barriers in your path. There were many times when I thought others were holding me back, only to dig deep inside and discover that I was holding myself back. It helped tremendously to have a spouse that saw things in me I did not see. He pushed me to move beyond my limiting beliefs.

Limiting beliefs keep us from the full, abundant life we were meant to live. We have all been guilty of falling victim to assumptions that have hindered us. We do this by making decisions based on unchallenged conclusions. For example, if you believe you can't be successful because you failed the first time you tried, you won't persevere. Trusting the false belief that failure defines you becomes a self-fulfilling prophecy.

In reality, every "successful" person will testify that failure is the first step to success! Another limiting belief is that you can't make a difference and that what you say and do doesn't really matter. This false belief will paralyze you into becoming a bystander in life as opposed to playing the important role you were created for.

On the other hand, if you believe the opposite to be true, you will actively pursue ways to make a difference and experience the joy of helping, serving, and engaging with others—a much more fulfilling way to live! I urge everyone who is reading this to challenge your limiting beliefs, quit assuming the worst, and quiet the negative self-talk that keeps you from pursuing greatness. Be warned that whether you think you can or you think you can't, you are correct every single time.

What You Believe Matters

Throughout the years, I've actually learned to identify my limiting beliefs instead of avoiding them. This takes maturity and self-awareness. But it's a true clarifying moment when you see the thing you hadn't seen ever before. It's a stark realization that there's a belief that needs to be reframed.

One limiting belief I fell victim to: the lie that I had to behave contrary to who I really am. I believed that if I was to be successful, I couldn't be authentic. I call this belief window "Act Like a Man." I did not have many female role models in my career. And I mistakenly thought I needed to fit in by acting like a man, diminishing my differences and why I was valued. My breakthrough moment was when I embraced my difference and reframed the critical importance of being my true and authentic self. Busting through this belief window gave me the freedom to be who I was. I was able to celebrate the fact that I was a woman instead of feeling inferior. When my belief changed, my actions changed as well. This newfound confidence enabled me to reach higher levels of success that benefitted not only myself but also my company.

A second limiting belief I fell victim to: "I can do this myself." I believed if I kept my head down, focused on working harder than anyone else and delivering good results, my work would speak for my value and potential. It took me years to decide that networking was not a self-serving activity, one I had no time for. Why were promotions being given to others, and why was my work not broadly recognized? Busting through this belief window gave me the freedom to see the importance of building strong networks and learning from mentors.

The power of mentorship was foreign to me. It was not until I lifted my head up to see that if I wanted to progress in my career, I needed a broad base of people who knew me, my value, and my work. I realized that I needed to study the characteristics which were respected and rewarded. And

I needed to articulate my personal leadership values and behaviors and to model them in my daily journey.

I became a student of successful leaders and the company culture. I assessed my gaps and asked individuals who could help me close those gaps to become my mentors. I learned that a mentorship relationship required accountability on both sides. It requires the following:

1. Mentees must pick mentors with purpose.

2. Mentees must set the meeting times, the frequency, and the agenda with their mentors.

3. Mentees must ask for what they need and then apply the lessons shared by their mentors.

4. Mentees must never abuse a mentor relationship by wasting their mentors' time, by not following up on their advice, and by not being deliberate in how they spend their time with their mentors

    Later, as I was able to be a mentor, I always started with four questions in a face-to-face discussion.

    a. Why do you want me as your mentor?

    b. What is the goal you want to achieve from this commitment?

    c. Will you act on the advice I share?

    d. Will you own the responsibility for follow-up and for scheduling future meetings? My belief is that mentees must have skin in the game. If the burden rests on mentors, mentees may never achieve what they truly want from this relationship.

I know that mentors and sponsors made a huge impact on my career. I can attribute many of the opportunities presented to me on the basis of the growth I learned from being molded by a mentor and for the specific feedback shared about how and what I contributed when promotion decisions were being discussed.

A third limiting belief I fell victim to: "That's Not What Girls Do."

Traditional female careers at that time were teaching and nursing. These are critically important and noble professions. But they were not my passion. When I chose retailing, there were not many store managers or merchant category directors who were women. If I was going to be a successful business leader, I was going to have to break through traditional roles.

This required me to start from the ground up. I began my career in the stores as a sales associate and a department manager. Moving up required relocation. Career growth required me to take risks and be open to change. My greatest opportunities were not the ones I expected. I took on new roles, laterally and promotionally, to expand my skill sets and to build a broad base of experience in the retail fundamentals.

I accepted many lateral opportunities to learn and hone a broad foundation in operations and merchandising before I started to see promotions and career advancement come my way. By being open to lateral roles, I was better prepared for the promotions. I was able to demonstrate mastery of the core retail fundamentals before entering the senior leadership ranks.

Every experience required me to jump into new roles before I was "ready." Each time I was successful in the new role, I was building my confidence and courage. I may never have discovered the importance of courage and confidence if I said no to stretch assignments and career moves along the way. Some roles were unexpected left turns, leaving me scarred and questioning my own capabilities. By far and away, most of the new roles were hard-right decisions that propelled me into opportunities far beyond my expectations. All of the roles made me the gracious and strong leader I am today. They required me to break through my old belief windows and explore what was possible.

Overcoming my fear of not being good enough took many years. I recall two moments when I realized that fear was behind me.

The first happened when I moved from Sam's Club to Walmart. I was asked to work with a new-to-Walmart Inc. EVP of the Global People Division. He had most recently served as the chief operating officer (COO) with a discount retailer, and I was a senior vice president trying to successfully move across divisions.

Lawrence Jackson was an impressive and intense senior leader who worked at Walmart for only a few short years. His impact was profound, not known to many because of the confidentiality of the leadership role he played in the company. I learned so much from him, and I am forever grateful for the impact he made on me.

When I received my first promotion on the Walmart U.S. side of the business, he dropped by to congratulate me: "I knew you were going to be OK when you stopped leading for me, as your boss, and you started leading for you." His comment was a profound moment, realizing that my accountability was to my authentic self and to the people I had the privilege to lead. I will never forget that lesson!

The second example I will share occurred several years later. I was asked to step in and lead the Walmart U.S. Talent Development function. The team had been restructured to report up to the newly appointed chief administration officer (CAO). He was tough as nails, a career lawyer who required excellence and precision in every work product produced. He was not easy to work for, and he did not have an early positive impression of me. But a turning point for our working relationship happened during my All Hands meeting where I introduced Tom Mars to my entire team. I was asking Tom questions about his background, his vision for Walmart U.S., and the role Talent Development would play in accomplishing that vision. Suddenly, he turned the tables and started asking me tough questions. The critical question he asked was, "Why do you think you are the right person to turn around this function and to lead this team?" It was a direct challenge, in front of the entire team.

My answer: "Because I am good enough! I am a seasoned senior leader who has the experience, vision, and courage to reshape the contribution of each member of this team and together deliver excellence. We are preparing associates across Walmart U.S. to excel in their jobs. I, and this team, are good enough."

Our relationship was forever stronger and one of mutual respect after that exchange. The team felt valued and enabled to contribute in a meaningful way. This had not happened for them in a long time.

You are good enough when you believe you are. Extraordinary accomplishments become the fruits of your belief.

Limiting Beliefs and Behaviors

What are your limiting beliefs? This exercise took me a bit of time to identify. Start with your career or choice of profession. Are you working in a role that is your passion? If not, what is your career passion?

Second, evaluate your presence. Are you showing up in your role, looking the part for the position one level above your current level? If not, what is stopping you?

Finally, evaluate how you spend and invest your time. Are you spending the bulk of your time on what is most important to you? If not, evaluate where you are spending your time and why.

Create a chart with three or four sections. Write down your limiting belief in column one. List the specific things that you thought or think to be true as components of that limiting belief in column two. This will be your longest list. In column three, write down how you want to behave once your break out of the limitation.

Keep the chart handy so you can add to it and practice daily your new behaviors in column three.

If you are facing a large change at work or at home, look up the IMA Reaction Patterns to Change Models (located in the back of this book).

Plot where you are on this change curve. Be honest!

Realize that success lies in getting through the emotions of change quickly and moving to integration.

I have used these Change Curve models in all of my years when I led Change Management at Walmart U.S. Identifying where you are on the curve and accepting that you should move quickly through each stage has helped many people realize that they are limiting themselves. Change is happening all around us. The more quickly you can adapt and find your place in the new reality, the more you will be invited to be a part of big changes and not feel as if you are a victim of change.

Chapter 4

THE MOST PROFOUND LEADERSHIP ROLE YET

"For me, being a mother made me a better professional, because coming home every night to my girls reminded me what I was working for. And being a professional made me a better mother, because by pursuing my dreams, I was modeling for my girls how to pursue their dreams."

—MICHELLE OBAMA, FORMER FIRST LADY OF THE UNITED STATES OF AMERICA

One of my early career-limiting beliefs was that your career is the most critical role you will have in life. I demonstrated little empathy for other roles or circumstances that got in the way of their role at work. I certainly did not value the role of being a parent. What I know now is that the role of a parent is far more important, fulfilling, and difficult. God has a way of giving you just what you need to learn and grow.

The birth of my daughter was an event I had never expected to come. I had been selfish as a child, as a young professional, as a sister, and as a spouse. I even gave speeches on never having children when doing media training. I was solely focused on my career, and I was so grateful to find a spouse who was committed to his profession and who had agreed not to have children and was willing to put me first.

When we were married, we said we would recommit each year. We wanted the reminder that marriage was not just a piece of paper but a lifelong commitment to each other. We were proud that we were DINKS (Dual Income, No Kids), with big dreams, and that we were both willing and able to take on any challenge in order to progress professionally.

Then at the age of forty-five, my husband woke up and said, "There has to be more to life! We need a child."

WHAT?

His statement rocked my world. We had been married seventeen years. We had so much more to achieve! I decided I would give it one try, and God said, *"Now is the time."*

My role at the time was that of senior vice president on the executive committee for a membership club chain. I was fortunate that I could take maternity leave and return to my position after eight weeks. As a career woman, maternity leave was important to me, and I planned to return to work quickly. What I didn't plan on was the company being sold just five months later!

My hope at the time was to have a healthy baby. But, in all honesty, before I had a child, I thought that raising a child would come in second to my work. I thought I was being the martyr by becoming pregnant. The truth was that I was scared to death. But I kept up my front of being the brave and sacrificial spouse in this marriage. To reward my sacrifice I told my husband I wanted a bottle of chilled, ready-to-serve Dom Pérignon at the foot of my hospital bed. That was far beyond any champagne we ever had before, and only appropriate, in my mind. After I gave birth, it was right there!

The day she was born, God gave my husband and me a perfectly healthy baby girl. He gave us a child born to immense love and opportunity. She is the greatest gift of joy I have ever known, and obviously today she is so important to me that I can't imagine life without her. God entrusted my husband and me with the great privilege and responsibility to raise an independent, productive member of society who would give back and make this world a better place. My husband did a really tremendous job, and we both helped shape and mold a remarkable young woman.

There is no greater responsibility than parenthood. It is a 24/7 responsibility, and I learned that it must have priority over my work. Our children will be the most rewarding and significant contribution you can make to society.

In addition, I learned that they are watching and listening to everything you say and do.

I want my daughter to have a healthy and mutually respectful marriage filled with love and true partnership. If you want that for your children, you have to be their role model. Our marriage may not have been perfect, but we did model the values of partnership, independence and love.

David was present for all our daughter's life events; I was present at the important events, but I couldn't be present at all. The key to being successful in this dilemma is communication. When it comes to your children, have them tell you what events are most important to them, and tell them when you can and cannot be present. Lift them up and encourage them. Teach them they can do anything! Then step back and watch them try.

Keep them safe, and provide the best that you can make available for them. Require them to work hard and to earn what they achieve. Do not give them everything and then expect them to be grateful. And teach them through role modeling the values and principles most important to you for your family.

Try to be consistent with your partner on what is acceptable and what is not to your children. They will play you and pit you against each other if you and your partner are not consistent.

I did not stay home with our daughter when she was sick, unless her illness was serious and she needed both parents present. I took my turn when my husband had commitments. I took her to work with me on Saturday mornings and some evenings after school. We both exposed her to our work, to our commitments, to my church, and to giving back in the community.

Kyndall attended many Saturday morning meetings until she grew up enough to desire to sleep in. She was exposed to a strong female role model, whether she liked it or not. I had a point of view on grades, fairness, how to be a good friend, and how to respect authority. I took her to church every Sunday, until she chose to stay home as a teenager in high school and to stay on the campus of the college she attended. One of my proudest days was the day she got baptized at the age of twenty-two, when she "returned" to church—a church she had selected with college friends who had exposed her to a relevant church and its teachings.

One of the best pieces of advice I learned was to establish a policy of "if you call, I will be there immediately. No questions asked." Kyndall used it only once, when she was helping a friend stay out of trouble and they needed to get out of a situation quickly. I did not ask questions, but she opened up immediately after she and her friend were safely home.

I learned to be her parent, her advisor, and her counselor—not her friend. She understands that I am tough because I love her.

I had to learn to accept her and truly discover who she was. I had to spend time getting to know her as a teenager and a young adult. I shared in the celebration of her as much as I disciplined her. I was not the fun parent. But I was there when she needed me, always, even if she does not remember it that way.

Kyndall is such a blend of David and me. "Green acres" did not screw her up. She is much more country than city. But she has an appreciation for different points of view, and she can reconcile the extremes. She is remarkable! And she is the best thing David and I ever did together.

My inflated perception of being the brave and sacrificial spouse changed when we made the decision to join Sam's Club/Walmart. It required a move from Denver, Colorado, to Bentonville, Arkansas. And the limited career opportunities for architects in this small, rural town led to the most sacrificial decision a parent can make. David chose to become a stay-at-home dad, long before this choice was more common. His sacrifice allowed me to focus on my career and gave me the freedom to take on roles which required travel and long hours.

In return, he asked for the opportunity to buy a horse and some land when we could afford to do so. Little did I know that our decision to buy just one horse and "some land" would become nineteen horses and a fully operational horse stables, named The Stables at LaDena Downs. David named the facility after my mother: a beautiful gesture, in loving respect for a key role model in our lives and out of respect to me.

His vision for this facility was to be a place where children, particularly girls, could learn confidence and responsibility. He had instructors and programs for children to ride and to learn how to care for their horses. To witness these young children in control of a 1,000-pound animal with a mind of its own was remarkable. The facility was a special place, built on a noble vision.

Today, the facility is as beautiful as ever. It still offers horse owners and children the opportunity to experience the therapeutic benefits of bonding with horses. It is a remarkable place to watch the joy and love develop between children and their horses. It is a place that brings joy to many, and I know David is proud that it is still changing lives.

The most profound leadership role yet is parenthood. It is the most influential role you play in your family. This discovery did not come naturally to me. But through many unexpected left turns and the belief in a higher calling for our lives, I am proud to no longer compartmentalize, but rather to blend.

Being Profound as a Parent

Disclaimer: I do not stake the claim to having been a great parent.

But I will share a few things that I found to be profound.

1. Read to your child early and often.

2. Declare up front if you will not be able to attend all their meets, performances, and events. Then ask them which ones are important to *them* for you to attend. Do not take on the guilt of missing moments, but be there for the ones that matter.

3. Do not confuse being a friend with being a parent. Your role is to protect, to provide, and to teach the boundaries.

4. Be present when you are present.

   "Encourage and support your kids because children are apt to live up to what we believe in them." Lady Bird Johnson, former First Lady of the United States

Chapter 5
LEADERSHIP IS ABOUT RELATIONSHIPS

"A boss creates fear, a leader confidence. A boss fixes blame, a leader corrects mistakes. A boss knows all, a leader asks questions."

—RUSSELL H. EWING

Relationships are at the core of everything we do. Whether you're an executive or an entrepreneur, it's the way you relate to humans on a face-to-face level that matters. How are your relationships with your clients, your prospects, and your tipping-point people? How are you leading the employees on your team, and what does leadership mean to you?

Even after the third time asking that question, you may not know the exact answer. But we can all describe what leadership is not. We've all had examples of forceful, aggressive, or dominant and controlling leaders. There was a time when a charismatic and forceful leadership style was often promoted as the way to lead. But leaders who have a servant mind-set are very different. They do not lead by manipulation or intimidation.

If leaders are delivering excellent results, but they are leaving bodies in their wake, they must *go!* Leaving dead bodies (ruined relationships, forgotten colleagues, and anyone you stepped on to get ahead) is no way to lead. It will be lonely at the top when you realize you have destroyed the most important elements of true success and lasting happiness. Relationships, reputation, and moral excellence will always be more valuable than worldly success.

What do you do if you're a brand-new leader?

The first step is to establish the vision, mission, and purpose for your team during your first 90 days, and *never* more than 120 days. Visualize them, write them down on paper, and share them often. Leaders write things down. Leaders put their aspirations and expectations down for them to share. Keep your aspirations and expectations to one page. And refer to that page often as you inspire performance and excellence. You can recalibrate as you go, but communicating clearly and quickly is imperative.

The next step is finding the right talent. Talent is vital to your success and the success of the team. I failed at this lesson early in my career. But the lesson kept repeating itself. I discovered that finding the right talent is one of the most critical responsibilities you have as a leader. Surround yourself with great talent. Identify talent needs quickly; fill your gaps and voids with someone better than the person who left and better than you. Never settle. Talent will always reflect on you! You will be defined by the talent you bring into an organization, the quality of that talent, their on-going success, and the number you promote. Be a talent contributor and not a talent user.

There are very few people who can do everything well; therefore, we need others to help us. There are many people who are embarrassingly unaware of their limitations and try to be a "jack of all trades, master of none." Successful people surround themselves with other successful people who all bring something unique to the table. This world would be a boring place if we all were created the same. Embrace the differences in others, and as you work together, you will find that success is inevitable, and you can celebrate each person's unique contribution. Be cautious to never fall into the comparison trap. Every job and position are important and needed for success. Separate yourself from that class system. There may be a hierarchy, but everyone is needed to get the job done and to build a thriving business.

Another thing I learned during my time in the executive ranks is to be bold with your ideas and quick to take action. Every award I received was for innovation and speed! I wasn't big on waiting and analyzing, because I valued results and knew the expectations were high. You've got to plan and prepare, but then there's a time to take definitive action.

Be a leader who reinvents your relevance and is decisive and swift to take action. In every new role, I had to study the team and put the right people into the right seats on the bus. If I would drag my feet on these talent decisions, I was highly criticized. It took me many years to learn this lesson and move with speed on talent.

I also learned that developing relationships across the organization was critically important—not just at the highest levels but across the organization and with those who are closest to the customer too. You don't have to be loved by everyone, but it's important to be respected. Relationships are everything, and the only way to develop them is to invest time in people. I led support functions for many years of my career. I quickly learned that my super power was to build relationships with the primary functions of the business. I built my influence and effectiveness skills by becoming a valued and trusted partner with operations and merchandising. Because the only way I could deliver results that improved the business was understanding the associates I was serving and then influencing the leaders to support and sponsor my solutions.

You may be saying right now to yourself, "But I don't like networking!" Or, "But I'm not in sales!" Even the CIO of a company has to be able to connect, to integrate and to network in order to achieve his or her objectives. It's not enough to have technical or strategic management skills.

Networking Is Critical

You've got to seek out ways to network, to grow, and to connect. You've got to work hard in order to always be seen as relevant and necessary. If you work hard but no one knows you, who do you think would get the promotion? The one who was known by many and their work was respected, or the one who worked so hard to get results that he or she never even spent time being known by others? If others don't know you, it would be difficult to make a positive judgement about you. Make time to connect and network.

My best example of connecting and networking goes back to the time when I was transitioning from Sam's Club to Walmart U.S. Very few leaders moved between the two large divisions. But when I was given the opportunity, I needed a sponsor to pave the way. I had the benefit of two sponsors— Lee Scott and Mike Duke.

Lee assigned me to help a new EVP of People assimilate into the company. Mike Duke asked me to be the liaison between McKinsey Consulting and the Walmart U.S. leadership team. I was able to successfully navigate from Sam's Club to Walmart U.S., where I served for the last eleven years of my tenure. There was no road map or proven formula to follow; I did successfully navigate on the basis of relationships.

I have had the privilege of working for four Walmart Inc. CEOs during my tenure, and all of them demonstrated servant-leadership qualities. Each were unique individuals; each CEO led the organization differently, but all of them led for the betterment our associates, our shareholders, and the growth of the company. While leading, all remained authentic and true to their values and led by example. The common thread and key to the success for each one was servant leadership.

Doug McMillon is a strong servant leader. Doug spends more than 25 percent of his time as the CEO touring all aspects of our vast business. He engages with the people, and he is being heralded as *the* Culture Champion of Walmart Inc. A significant amount of time is spent by leaders across the business touring stores, clubs, and DCs (distribution centers). In that process of touring, they ask associates to walk along with them. It's a teaching opportunity every time—and that's not just the CEO; it's the segment president, the country president, and the senior leadership in each of the segments. This culture of respect, service, excellence, and integrity impacted the way I personally evolved as a leader.

When I led membership marketing and logistics, I spent three days on the road every week, traveling and touring the clubs and the DCs. And when I toured those facilities, I always learned from the experience and saw firsthand numerous examples of servant leadership. Not only were associates included, but they were also invited to walk alongside their leaders. In doing so, their actions revealed the importance of a relationship by valuing people over position. In turn, the leaders' associates were becoming more committed to the company, as bonds were formed, while, at the same time, knowledge was shared.

I love that this leadership style benefits all involved, including all levels of associates. By choosing to be actively engaged, asking questions, and listening, leaders are able to get a real understanding of what is going on in the company. Business acumen, associate engagement, how well the leaders knew their members, the question, "Who's that Member?" were being evaluated and celebrated with each visit. It's a really great way to teach but also to develop a reputation for servant leadership, for the store, as well as the facility as a whole. It is one of the key attributes that I think has made Walmart so successful. The leaders at Walmart manage each store, each facility, each club, and each DC, one location at a time.

You can't get caught up with the numbers. Walmart has more than 4,500 stores in the United States. If you thought about it as a whole, you would never be able to make any personal imprint on an organization of such size. Every CEO had a major impact on my development as a professional. I came into the company being a student of the culture and a student of each CEO.

It was one of David Glass's lessons to all of us: *Don't get hung up on the size of the company or your segment. The best way to impact the business is one store, one club, and one DC at a time.*

I would say that one of my best examples of servant leadership happened at Sam's Club, and it is still going on today. During National Small Business Week, each member of management (such as the CEO, the senior executives, the operations leaders, and club management teams), would go into a member's place of business and work. We each would do the job of the staff in that business for one-half to one working day. We were each assigned to one of the top business members, and we would go work with them. Then we would come back, and, in our leadership meetings, we would talk about the lessons we experienced, what was working, and what we must change.

It helped us understand what our business members needed—because we had worked alongside them, we walked in their shoes, and we listened to their needs. In each club, we would do this quarterly, but, at least once a year, the CEO and his or her leadership team would be working in a member's place of business. It's hard for pride or arrogance to take root in leaders who are willing to step out from their position and do whatever is required. By maintaining a teachable spirit, we were all able to connect with others, while at the same time responsibly using our positions to make necessary improvements that benefitted all.

Think about the humble mind-set it would take in order to walk a day in the shoes of a Walmart or SAM's Club customer, member, or associate and learn about that job and ways you could improve things. Servant leaders begin with a humble mind-set.

One CEO, Doug, has a personal goal of responding to every email that he receives within twenty-four hours. It's unbelievable, and he did so when he was a chief merchant. He did so when he was the CEO at SAM's Club and the CEO of the International Division, and he stills does so now. His character and commitment didn't change, even though his position did. He is always thoughtful, and even if the email is short, it always reflects that he has read it. Little things like this make a huge impact.

If he thinks that an email needs a follow-up, he will copy a team member for follow-up. He also walks the floor of the home office every week, sometimes more than once a week. Every one of the CEOs I served did exactly the same thing. It was impressive and memorable when the CEO stopped by your desk or office just to chat. The CEOs choose to do this, and it doesn't go unnoticed, because their presence is appreciated by all. As they travel through the halls, meeting associates, they ask, "What is working? What is not working? How is morale?"

"What's successful? What's not successful?" These are questions they will ask, truly probing for honest answers freely shared without reprimand.

They would just drop in to ask questions and listen to what you are working on right now. They would drop into the Sam's Club building and talk to the membership team to learn about membership growth. You never know when they were going to show up (that in itself is a great leadership style; associates are always anticipating their arrival on any given day). And it is wonderful when your CEO just drops in, because, for a few minutes, you get an audience with him or her. It is a terrific way for CEOs to listen and learn about the businesses. They meet you where you are.

When I was on the Walmart U.S. team, I worked for three segment CEOs who utilized open forums for communication and feedback. They held town hall meetings every single month. They would broadcast each meeting out to our divisional offices, regional offices, and market offices so that we could include our field leadership.

Leaders who do not understand servant leadership would not even consider this open forum of communication. That is to their detriment.

One thing I've learned is to always respect others, no matter their role or stature in life. Excellence requires doing more every year to stay relevant and bring innovation. Everyone has a different way of leading.

When you are a servant leader, serving others is your greatest reward! When we place our focus on others rather than on exercising power and control, we become effective leaders that others choose to follow. Servant leaders model action and therefore are change agents in the world.

A few years after my husband's death, I was offered the opportunity to take a position in Brazil. Susan Chambers and Doug McMillon asked me to consider the position, and because I trusted them and their judgment, I moved forward with WebEx interviews, speaking with the region EVP and the country president. I liked what I learned and began to get excited about the opportunity. However, I was still discovering who I was after David's death. When you look at life and have to recalibrate who you are, things are often unclear. I went home to talk to my daughter about the opportunity, and she completely broke down. She said it would be as if she had lost both her parents because I would be so far away.

The amazing part of this story is how each leader responded when I had to pull my name out of consideration.

My decision was treated with care and respect. I was never made to feel pressure or treated as if the decision not to pursue the opportunity was the end of my career. The pinnacle act of true leadership was a hand-written note I received from Doug: "Dear Celia, you have made the right decision for you and Kyndall. You would have contributed a great deal to the team in Brazil. Thank you for considering the opportunity. You are a great mom!"

I was so emotional when I read his note, I immediately called him to say thank you, and, during the call, I was still emotional. He demonstrated servant leadership at its core, truly showing care and concern for the betterment of others. I was the grateful recipient, and his behavior was a true display of what real leadership looks like.

What does it mean to be excellent? It means to continuously improve, to focus on lifelong learning. It doesn't mean you have to be perfect. It just means a commitment to continually push through fears, overcome obstacles that may seem like failure to you, and have faith that you'll come out strong on the other side. Never rest in maintenance. Never be satisfied with your own "press." Reinvent yourself, your leadership, and your objectives every year.

Don't make the mistake of resting in past performances; this is complacency. Work hard to never become complacent. Challenge yourself to grow and learn with every opportunity.

When I coach other leaders about servant leadership, I encourage them and say, "You have to stay in training mode, always improving and getting stronger. Every conversation, presentation, and work product, create an opportunity for feedback. Welcome it and reflect on how you can apply it."

Find ways of strengthening yourself and your
relationships, without overpowering those around you. In
business or in our personal lives, relationships are at the
core of our ability to influence and inspire. We learn what
traits we admire and those we don't. Be the mentor that you
wanted. Servant leaders start by understanding the needs
of those they serve. And then they ask what they can do
to solve your greatest need. This mind-set is an important
competitive advantage!

Leader Characteristics That Followers Admire

The most frequent responses, in order of mention, from extensive surveying by Kouzes, Posner, and Schmidt, published in *The Leadership Challenge* are:

Integrity – Is truthful, is trustworthy, has character, has conviction.

Competence – Is capable, is productive, is efficient.

Forward-looking – Is decisive, provides direction, sets or selects a desirable destination toward which the organization should head.

Inspiring – Is enthusiastic, is energetic, is positive about the future.

Put it all together – **Credibility:** perceived trustworthiness, expertise, and dynamism.

How would your followers describe you?

Ask yourself the following introspective questions:

1. How would your followers describe you as a leader?
2. How would you describe your leadership characteristics?
3. Do the two descriptions match?
4. Ask for feedback on how you would be described from respected sources. Use this feedback as a inspiration to strengthen yourself and the important relationships in your life.

Work to build strong and positive relationships with your team. This investment will help them grow as a professional and is vital to the success of an organization.

Chapter 6

CULTURE IS THE GREAT DIFFERENTIATOR

"I used to believe that culture was 'soft,' and had little bearing on the bottom line. What I believe today is that culture has everything to do with our bottom line, now and into the future."

—Vern Dorsh, author,
Wired Differently

Every organization has a distinct culture, whether it deliberately attempts to create it or not. Culture matters more than many leaders understand. Some leaders are more focused on getting their business started and growing it to scale; they assume their culture will develop itself. Leaders too often put culture on the sidelines.

But culture matters.

A culture can be healthy or toxic, sustainable or divisive, strong or weak. A healthy, sustainable, strong company culture has a direct impact on the results. An evaluation of company cultures, published by John Kotter and James Heskett, found that, over an eleven-year period, companies with healthy cultures had a 682 percent average increase in sales versus 166 percent in companies with unhealthy cultures. There were also stock increases of 901 percent versus 74 percent. These percentages prove that excellent business strategy requires a great company culture and that ineffective business strategies are directly impacted by a poor culture.

Walmart's secret sauce has long been its culture. It is alive, thriving through many changes in leadership and strategy. It is current and relevant, and it is a draw for talent in today's workplace. That has not happened by chance. The culture is well documented, hangs on the walls of every store, club, DC and home office building. More important, it is lived out in leadership and associate behaviors, measured often and taught through storytelling and celebrations.

A brilliant strategy can fail if it is not coupled with a strong company culture. In fact, culture trumps strategy!

To understand the culture in your organization ask yourself the following questions:

How do you know if you have a culture that needs to be redefined? What are your values? What is your why? What are the behaviors you reward?

In my final role at Walmart Inc., I was leading the Global Culture team, focused on our culture initiatives all across the globe. It was full circle for me, because I came to be a student of the culture and chose to join Sam's Club/ Walmart to add to the culture. It was the most tremendous honor to be leading culture across the globe as one of my last assignments in the company.

What did I learn through leading culture? That culture trumps strategy. It means that an organization can have a brilliant strategy that fills an important need in society. It can be inspiring in what it is trying to accomplish. But if the values, the behaviors, and how the work gets done do not line up with the culture, then the mission cannot be fulfilled.

Strategy is the WHAT; culture is the HOW. Strategy is not sustainable without culture.

The best strategic ideas mean nothing in isolation. When you just have strategy, you are just engaging the organization's head. But success requires engagement of the head and the heart. If you can engage the organization's heart, then you get the whole picture. That kind of culture is what brings to life an organization that has engaged employees who will go above and beyond to support their company. You simply cannot achieve optimal success without a strong culture.

What's the culture of your company?

Culture is all about behaviors. Your core values should remain the same over time. But it is important to adapt your approach and the behaviors you promote and reward to remain current and relevant to a changing customer base, economic environment, and generational relevance. Refreshing the behaviors that you will use to evaluate how your culture comes to life should be done on a regular basis. It can change the course of your relevance and create new opportunities for taking your brand to a new level.

An example of the power a culture can have on strategy and reputation occurred when Lee Scott gave his Twenty-First-Century Leadership Speech at Walmart. His message and how he empowered the people within as well as external support for Walmart was transformative. And he used this platform to convert those who may not have been supporters to become advocates. Through one simple speech, we began a journey into sustainability and social responsibility that has changed the course of history for Walmart and its people.

Let's start with how Walmart associates at all levels brought sustainability awareness and education to life. One of the requirements that Lee Scott implemented was to have his direct reports go on a "sustainability trip" every year. I had the opportunity to go on several of those trips. My first trip was related to underwater deep-sea research and sustainable fishing practices. We visited the underwater science laboratory off the coast of Key Largo, Florida, where scientists do impressive marine research. We learned a great deal about the varieties of fish we sell in our stores and clubs. We learned which fish would be better choices for us to sell on the basis of their impact on the environment.

On the second trip, we focused on water conservation and infrastructure in California. Our experience was a river-raft excursion on the Sacramento River, the principal river of northern California. We learned about the water crisis there and developed a point of view on ways we could help the state with their water emergencies and needs.

The third sustainability trip was to San Francisco, where I helped design our global Personal Sustainability Practices (PSP) engagement program. We ignited the engagement of 2.2 million associates in how they could adopt new behaviors and impact sustainability at home, at their facility, and in their community. It was a way to take sustainability from a corporate objective and personalize it for local associates, at stores, clubs, and DCs across the world. We created the PSP initiative. What we unleashed was the ability of every associate to make an impact!

We created the opportunity to make a huge imprint on water conservation, on air quality, on recycling, on sustainable gardening, on restoring community green space, and on other daily-life elements that we often take for granted. We created PSP teams in every facility and watched as our amazing associates rallied to become good stewards of our planet. We did not know if we could bring sustainability, education, and impact to an individual level. But our associates exploded the impact made locally and proved that sustainability *is* a personal issue.

Once we began this PSP initiative, it grew like wildfire. We discovered a way to ignite action around the globe! Can you imagine? When you bring awareness to a topic that affects millions, it can bring the attention of a million more. One of the most rewarding initiatives to design and to implement had exploded the impact being made locally and globally. Never underestimate the power of your people! They will amaze and inspire you if you let them. This lesson is a great reminder for what is possible. It is a great example of how a strong culture can change the course of your relevance with generations and naysayers. Today, Walmart is a strong leader in sustainability practices and impact. They are a corporate leader in social responsibility and a critical partner in all the communities they serve.

Culture is all about behaviors. And what we do matters.

It really matters that you don't get caught up in the enormity of it all, but focus on the small ways you can create impact.

Servant Leadership at the Associate Level

One of the most critical ways to keep your culture alive and well is practicing open communication. The "open door" is a process and a leadership practice focused on open communication and the voice of our associates. If associates have a concern or if they feel as if they haven't been treated fairly, they can take the concern to management without fear of retaliation. If the associates don't like the decision, they can take it to a higher level of management, possibly all the way up to the CEO. We empower the local leadership to first investigate and resolve the concern and make the right decision, but we guide the local leaders in their questions and provide council as needed. Decisions can go in favor of the associate. Or they can go in favor of management. But access to leadership is a critical component to a thriving work environment at Walmart.

I have witnessed dozens of examples where decisions, made through the open-door process, were overturned by senior leadership. Not that management had done a bad job or had made a bad decision. But if there was gray in the decision, leaders often made the decision in favor of the associate. They wanted to give the associate a second chance. Open-door concerns rarely go all the way up to the CEO. Any level of leadership can overturn an open-door decision if they have the justification to show why it is the right thing to do. Leaders have the discretion to overturn decisions just to show that the open-door policy works for our associates. There would be no belief in open communication if every decision was made in favor of management. So we consciously choose to overturn outcomes to reinforce to our associates that the open-door policy works.

Most of all, we train our teams on the open-door spirit and process. We take corrective action if an environment of retaliation exists. It is important that a company maintain an environment of open communication. We teach associates and leaders what the open-door process is all about. It is fundamentally different than "open-door policies" I have seen in other companies. It is taught, it works, and it creates an environment of partnership.

My personal example is one where the open-door process was used because of a misstep that I had made. I was promoting an individual to join my People Leadership team at Sam's Club. There was a very talented, up-and-coming female lawyer, and I wanted her to be part of my team. She talked to her supervisor and got permission to be interviewed. I even had a signed requisition from her supervisor that said, "Yes, we could have a conversation with her."

We conducted our interviews and selected her as our top candidate. I extended her the job offer, and she accepted. Excitedly, I told my team she would be joining us! But that never happened.

You see, I skipped an important step. Her boss chose to use the open-door process and take his concern to David Glass, CEO of Walmart Inc. Her boss said, "How can this be allowed? I have never once talked to Celia about this." We were both senior VPs. So the respect that I did not show him was that I didn't pick up the phone and have a conversation with him about the role I had to offer and my intention to extend her an offer. I should have given him the personal courtesy and respect of communicating with him first.

My decision to promote her was overturned. David Glass ruled that there were bigger opportunities for her and that I had made a misstep. I had to go back to my team, to admit my mistake, and to inform them that the search was back open. In the end, I didn't get to have this bright individual on my team.

It was hard for me to swallow my misstep, because I am truly aligned with the company's values. But as I learned, if you make a misstep, you need to own it. I skipped a very important step—simple as that! I went to my team, and I let them know that we didn't get to have this amazing talent on our team. Honestly, I was crushed. I truly thought I would lose the respect of my team. But it was just the opposite. I gained their respect because I was transparent. They saw me step up and own my misstep. They saw me use this as a teachable moment, and it made me human and approachable.

I dreaded getting up in front of my team, but I had a great mentor who advised that the best thing you can do is build trust with your team. Don't sweep your mistakes under the rug. People respect you more when you own up to your mistakes. When we try to hide behind our excuses, we will only excel at being good excuse makers who ultimately become poor leaders that no one will follow.

Because I refused to make an excuse for my behavior, the level of trust between my team and me increased exponentially.

Another example of open communication and trust building was lived out through our Annual Shareholder Week events. I have had the privilege to go to many shareholder meetings for the last twenty years. Walmart's shareholder meeting is as much a cultural event as it is a traditional business meeting with the shareholders and the financial community. There is nothing traditional

about a Walmart shareholder meeting! We invite 20,000
associates, shareholders, and investors to attend our annual
shareholder meeting. It takes place in the Bud Walton
basketball arena located on the University of Arkansas
Fayetteville campus. And we house our associates in the
dormitories on campus for the full week leading up to the
shareholder meeting.

In the earlier years at Sam's Club, we would host a
picnic. It was an appreciation for those associates selected
to attend. One associate from every club is selected to
attend on behalf of all the associates in their facility. It
is a cultural celebration, with activities throughout the
week, culminating on Friday morning with the official
shareholder meeting.

We spend the week engaged in education and
entertainment activities. We maximize the associates' time
while they are in Northwest Arkansas.

Each business segment spends time developing
engagement activities. At Sam's Club, one event is a picnic
with leadership. We also do exchanges with merchants,
membership, and the People Division. Each associate
represents one of those functions in his or her club. We
listen to the club associates working in our function, and we
implement changes on the basis of their recommendations.
We invest a day in listening and learning from the people on
the front line.

Leadership moments were special. We would have
lines of associates that would want to get their picture
taken with the leaders. Most popular were the CEO and
the Executive VP of Operations, because they were the
top of their chain of command. But we would all show up
to meet and appreciate our field team. We would stay out
there until all associates had gotten their photos with the
executives of their choice. We believed that all associates

who took the time to stand in line were important; therefore, it was an honor to have our pictures taken with them. They would go back to their respective clubs and tell stories about their experiences, about being part of the remarkable activities during the week, and about what they learned.

Many times, during my club visits, I would see a picture of the associate that he or she took with the head merchant, with the head of operations, with me, or with the CEO. The picture would always make me smile. The associate and I would spend time talking about what that experience meant to them. This was a way to stay close to the associates in a big company—by creating individual connections. Relationships are key in servant leadership.

At Walmart U.S., we hosted a huge pep rally. We asked the associates to submit questions they would like to have answered. They would line up at the microphones to ask their questions, give home office their feedback, and get a response directly from the senior leadership team. The international team does this as well. They invest a day on teaching, reinforcing, and celebrating our company culture. They highlight key initiatives from each country, and then get a chance to ask questions of the leadership at the end of the day. The shareholder week and the open-door process are just two examples of how we promote servant leadership—giving us a chance to serve and lift up each associate.

The Walmart Inc. CEO attends every business segment's year-beginning meeting (YBM), and the holiday/fall manager's meeting. The CEO shares a company message, but they also walk the merchandising floor with the field managers—listening, hearing feedback, and sharing the big picture of what's going on in the company. In addition, the CEO attends nearly every country's YBM. It is a huge time investment that the CEO makes, but it matters when building relationships and trust.

Walmart Inc. operates four different business segments—Walmart U.S., Sam's Club, International, and E-Commerce, but it's our culture that binds us altogether. We are all connected as a whole. These moments were an opportunity for David Glass to talk about growth and taking our company global. Or for Lee Scott to talk about supercenter growth and our impact on the environment. Or for Mike Duke to talk about new formats, such as the neighborhood market and global growth. And for Doug McMillon to talk about growth and our transformation to become a digital and bricks-and-mortar retail leader. It has always been important to invest the time and personal messages that keep our people informed and united as a whole. It matters!

A company's core values must stand the test of time. But the behaviors and what you reward must evolve and be relevant to future generations and ready to serve the changing customer needs. You simply cannot achieve sustained business success without a strong culture. It's in the values you hold to be true and in the bright lines of right principles for any organization. Walmart is a role-model corporation when it comes to a healthy, sustained, and strong company culture.

Culture Matters

Four fundamental truths based on my experience as a champion for culture:

1. Your why is your strongest position.

    •   Can you effectively communicate your why? If not, take time to think about your why and how you best communicate it internally and externally. Brands connect at an emotional level, not at an intellectual level.

    •   This is true for companies and individuals. What is your personal why?

2. The best strategic ideas mean nothing in isolation.

    •   If your strategy conflicts with how people believe, behave, or make decisions, it will fail. Does your company culture conflict with your strategy, or does it support it? What is your assessment?

    •   Success requires engagement of the head and the heart. How are you engaging the head and the heart of the people around you?

3. Culture is all about behaviors.

    •   Although your core values should remain the same over time, it's important to adapt the approach of your organization based on a changing customer base, economic environment, and generational relevance.

    •   How have you adapted to make yourself relevant within your organization?

4. Culture must be lived out.

- Living out your core values starts from the top and has a ripple effect.

- What are your core values? How are you living them out in your daily behavior?

Chapter 7
UNEXPECTED LEFT TURNS

"Accept the challenges so that you may feel the exhilaration of victory."

—General George S. Patton

Our lives and careers are simply a series of unexpected left turns that take us from one season to the next. At times, they can seem like insurmountable challenges, while at other times, they may seem like golden opportunities. This concept of "unexpected left turns" may have been the reason you picked up this book. When I was doing the research with my readers, I discovered that what they wanted most was advice on how to manage their leadership journey in the midst of life's and career's greatest challenges. Somewhere in life, my readers had taken an unexpected left turn. They felt stuck or caught in a rat race. They wanted real-life advice and examples of how to navigate and stay on course.

This chapter is dedicated to unpacking the concept of life and career-overwhelming challenges. I am going to share with you ten of the most common unexpected left turns you may personally or professionally face, along with some practical tools to help you grow as a leader.

Toxic Workplace Culture

No one joins an organization knowing it's a toxic environment. Instead, most new hires eagerly anticipate a bright future, excited to transition beyond a typical eight-to-five job into embracing a special and rewarding career. Unfortunately, however, all too often, after the honeymoon fades, the true nature of the company is revealed, and you uncover its cultural shortcomings. Elements of distrust, gossip, burnout, and fatigue are just a few examples of the behaviors that exist in a toxic workplace.

How to deal with a toxic workplace:

To more effectively navigate this unexpected challenge, actively probe and understand the facts of the situation. In other words, pause, take a step back, and discover whether your workplace is indeed toxic or whether the toxicity comes from your closest professional surroundings. You may discover that your immediate supervisor is not living out the core values of the company yet the company's values remain strong in other executives, team members, or departments.

You also need to consider the following questions: What are the facts? What organizational values are commended and rewarded? What leadership qualities are highlighted and encouraged? What do those around you stand for when no one's looking? If the answers to these questions are nonexistent or, worse, negative, it may be time to consider an exit strategy.

Job Loss

There are few words to describe the devastation that comes with a job loss. One day you're in, and the next day you're out, and there's nothing you can do to change it. It's during these unexpected challenges you may feel as though you've lost complete control. Because of circumstances outside your scope of influence, including company results or organizational mergers, sometimes a professional departure may actually have very little to do with you personally.

How to deal with job loss:

The quickest way to navigate through this terrain is to regain your balance, take back control, and invest in yourself. This process begins with pursuing your next career opportunity, networking, going back to school, or even equipping yourself with additional skills that are highly marketable through training or coaching.

Misaligned Values

I can't emphasize enough the importance of knowing your values as an individual. When you have a core set of personal values, you have something that no one can take from you. You know what you stand for, and you demonstrate the values you expect a company to exhibit. For me, respect for the individual is a core principle. If a colleague mistreats another, or worse, a subordinate, I know respect is not part of their core values.

How to deal with misaligned values:

First, do your homework, if you haven't already, by researching the company's core values. It's important to understand the heart of these principles and how the company expects them to play out day-to-day in the organization. The values should be extremely positive and written on every department wall. Still, if the behaviors are not at all consistent, that's when you have misalignment.

Note that misaligned company values are different than having a bad boss with bad values, which I'll address in the next point. When your boss's values are off, you stay to determine a way to become the change you want see. When the entire company's values are off, you transition out and take your skills where they will be most valued.

Bad Boss

Having a bad boss doesn't grant you a one-way ticket for leaving the company. Bad leaders come and go, but the way you choose to influence the situation will leave a lasting thumbprint. If I had bailed out after my first bad boss, I would have missed a remarkable career. I would have missed the opportunity to make a difference.

How do deal with a bad boss:

Instead of leaving, choose to be the change. Figure out ways to help with the boss's emotional intelligence, self-awareness, and desire to lift up others.

If time goes on and there is still no change or sign of improvement, find another place within the organization where you can actively use your gifts and skills. It's important to remember not to compromise your behavior but embody the shining example you desire to see in both your organization's leadership and culture.

Family Illness or Loss

The need to manage family illness, or worse, a loss, can feel like a sudden jolt that can quickly consume your entire life. There is an immediate and automatic mental shift that takes place when taking care of a family member. This sudden shift requires you to balance more than you typically would, forcing you to reprioritize your schedule and expectations both personally and professionally.

When my mom was diagnosed with breast cancer, my dad made the decision to be the caretaker the entire way through. In his mind, it was not even a choice to separate himself from the situation. The same is true for a loss; depending on the situation, you must always make the decision on how you respond.

How to deal with a family illness or loss:

Dealing with family illness or loss starts with choosing to face into your responsibilities and having a clear understanding of what all it will require from you. This might mean putting your career on a temporary hold. For some, the hold is a couple of weeks; for others, it could be years. Still, having the willingness to do that gracefully and appropriately for the circumstances will help tremendously.

One of the critical pieces to face is also finding a way to secure yourself. You have to find that way to protect yourself and not lose yourself. In other words, don't give into the negativity, but find a way to maintain your sense of self-awareness, find your peace, and find your direction. Doing so will help give you a better sense of direction throughout the process.

While most of us jump to the conclusion that unexpected left turns are negative, they're not always, and they can actually be exciting and positive. Being open to embrace the positive opportunities that may come your way is just as important as preparing yourself for how you're going to handle negative challenges. Everything in life is a choice, which is why it's important to be open to saying, "Yes," to positive opportunities.

Throughout my career, I had to find a way to say, "Yes," even when I was given opportunities that others didn't take or didn't want. Saying, "Yes," propelled me to progress my career broadly and rapidly. It's easy to say, "Oh no, I won't move there," or, "Oh no, I won't 'waste my time' with lateral job assignments." However, finding your way to yes is probably one of the best skill sets you can ever develop.

One of my early career decisions to deviate from my charted path was to pursue a buyer position. My degree was in fashion merchandising, but my career had taken me into the operations side of business. Despite the likelihood of promotion to store manager, I wanted to discover if merchandising was my true career calling. I walked into the office and said, "I'd like to give this a shot." What did I discover? I wasn't a great merchant, and I lacked the skills to be a great buyer. I discovered my obvious strengths were working with people, which led me to actively pursue a new role in human resources. Thankfully, this discovery launched the beginning of a successful and rewarding career.

Embracing unexpected left turns is all about being open to different opportunities and having a belief window of saying, "How can I get to yes in this situation?"

Unexpected Leadership Role

The excitement of a new career or life opportunity is something that can be quite flattering and validating. The big promotions can often serve as a platform to demonstrate your traits as a leader.

How to leverage a new leadership role:

Go into the opportunity with a strong sense of your strengths and assets. If you are a visionary with a strategic mind-set, think through how you will narrow your focus on taking your team or business to new levels of success. You will also need to think through how to build a team that helps you execute the details effectively and get things done. If you are more of a practitioner in nature, expose yourself to opportunities that will equip you and your team to develop innovative business strategies.

You should also always be prepared for the next opportunity by the way you show up in your day-to-day behaviors. For example, Sarah Thomas was the first female NFL official. At a recent conference, she shared her story of the day when she got the call from NFL executives that they had a job opening for an official. She had been equipping herself all along to have the skills needed to take on a big job leap, and, suddenly, it arrived!

The best part about her story is that it wasn't about her capabilities and how she actually made game calls. Instead, it was about how she handled herself on the field. That's how the NFL executives knew she was ready for the next level. How you handle yourself and how you show up every day cause others to determine when you're ready for that next big step.

Parenting

Having children is the greatest gift God provides us. The most important role we can play in life is to mold and shape a healthy, independent, and contributing adult. However, despite the joys that come with parenting, it's a 24/7 responsibility. There are curve balls at every turn that force you to slow down, manage stress and adversity, and recalibrate. You can't control when your child's going to be sick and you have to take off work. You can't fully prepare for the various stages of dependencies—from infancy to early childhood and all the way through college. But you can become a better leader every step of the way, which in turn makes you a better parent.

Before I had children, I was incredibly single-minded in my focus and approach to my life and career. Little did I know that having my first and only child would change the way I approached life and leadership altogether. Amidst lunchtime visits and toddler dates, I soon realized that having a meaningful and healthy relationship with my daughter was the biggest win I could achieve in life. Kids change you.

How to identify as a parent within your career:

One of the most influential ways to lead at work is to make hands-on family involvement a part of the culture and the conversation. Such involvement could be as simple as having photos of you and your family in your office and scheduling ongoing lunches with your child at school. You may also need to find ways to work remotely when your family needs you or find ways to accomplish your job that doesn't require you in the office each day.

As a leader, doing this sets a tone for your team that it's OK to blend work and life, as needed. It also let's your team see a more personal side of you through your family, and it will communicate the importance of putting your family first in work and life.

I'll never forget when I saw a female executive at my company announce to an entire room of associates that she needed to end the meeting promptly at four o'clock to go watch her daughter play basketball in a regional playoff. She did it unapologetically in front of everyone and made a point to say, "*Yes*, it's important to be there for your kids!"

Although I didn't always make it to every recital or game, I was extremely intentional about sitting down with my daughter and asking her what event was most important for me to attend. Having that conversation and finding out from your children is critical. If I did have to miss other events, I would call her as soon as the event was over and celebrate her achievement.

Moving to a New Place

I'll never forget the time my husband and I decided to move from the Colorado to Northwest Arkansas. It was an experience that, at the time, I was unsure of, but when I finally got adjusted, I soon realized it was an amazing place to live and raise a family.

The reality of moving to a new place can be exciting and stressful at the same time, stretching you in unexpected ways. However, the way you choose to make the most out of where you are will shape what's to come.

How to leverage moving to a new place:

When you make the hard-right decision to be fully present in your community, you will get exposed to a lot of leadership opportunities. Whether it's networking at professional events or joining a community cause, building a sense of community for yourself the moment you arrive is essential for gaining momentum in your life and career.

It's important to also be sensitive toward a trailing spouse. In my case, my husband was the trailing spouse (supporting my career goals first) when we moved. Despite the uncertainty of a new place, he made a point to get involved with the city chamber and helped lead efforts to build a recreational trail system that transformed the quality of life in Northwest Arkansas. Hundreds of thousands of people enjoy the trails to this day, and the trails continue to expand across the region.

When your trailing spouse is happy, you're happy. Getting your spouses involved quickly in a way that matters and makes them feel a sense of purpose is key. It's part of that formula for success when you and your spouse are moving to a new place, establishing roots, and building new relationships.

Career Breakthrough

Have you ever felt stuck in a job until suddenly it morphs into a career you love? Unlike promotions, which are somewhat predictable, a career breakthrough serves as a game-changing milestone that can happen in an instant or over years of hard work.

When a breakthrough does happen, it's important to make the most out of the opportunity.

How to leverage a career breakthrough:

First, take time to really celebrate the achievement. Again, a moment like this seldom happens; therefore, celebrating allows you to look back on what it took to get there. Make sure to celebrate your achievement with close friends, family, and the loved ones who matter in your life and who can cheer you on in the moment.

You'll want to also have clear goals for how this role will enhance and affect your well-being. Does it allow you to lead authentically? Will it increase your ability to influence in new ways? If so, how? Will it grant you a better quality of life? Be sure to jot these thoughts down so you stay centered and always remember why you first accepted the role.

Personal Breakthrough

A personal breakthrough occurs when you reach a personal achievement in your life that shows you what you're truly made of. This is different than a career breakthrough because it's about the character building you develop over time that gives you that extra layer of skin you didn't have before. It's also something you may experience during any of the previous unexpected left turns.

How to leverage a personal breakthrough:

Whether through journaling or enjoying the achievement with a close loved one, find a more intimate way to celebrate this kind of win. Sometimes an achievement like this can disguise itself through battle wounds. Still, the act of celebrating can make the experience that much sweeter.

Second, use your new sense of self-awareness as a strength to propel you forward. More important, don't let any of your past strongholds prevent you from being the best version of yourself. Past strongholds may look like negative friendships or relationships, bad habits, or negative ways of thinking. Counteract those things with positive replacements, and you will experience a sense of true significance. Note that this may take years or months of hard work, but remain committed to it! It's worth it!

Remember that there is great value to your growth and leadership in all of these life changes. Unexpected left turns are a core part of pursuing your calling as a leader and living a life well-led.

Let's Unpack Your Unexpected Left Turns

1. How would you describe your leadership journey as you've grow in your career?

2. What are some ways you've felt stuck in work or life?

3. What are your greatest leadership pain points right now?

Here are the ten most common unexpected left turns:

- Toxic workplace culture
- Job loss
- Misaligned values
- Bad boss
- Family illness or loss
- Unexpected leadership role
- Parenting
- Moving to a new place
- Career breakthrough
- Personal breakthrough

a. Is there one you are experiencing now?

b. Write down the tips or ideas that you will apply tomorrow to help you build a life of significance.

c. Post on my website at celiaswanson.com feedback about how you have applied them and how they have helped.

d. Learn from other readers on how they are successfully navigating unexpected left turns as they post their feedback at celiaswanson.com.

Remember that there is great value to your growth and leadership in all of these life changes. Unexpected left turns are a core part of pursuing your calling as a leader and living a life well-led .

Chapter 8
BE KNOWN

*"It's not what you gather in life,
but what you scatter in life that tells
the kind of life you've lived and
the kind of person you are."*

—HELEN WALTON

Influence is a gift. Influence and ego are two different things. Ego is a roadblock to influence. Ego puts the focus on the person; influence puts the focus on the outcome. With influence, you can change lives. If you don't have influence, you can't.

In two recent conversations, I was asked for my advice on expanding leadership influence into the community and how to get started. These were two senior leaders in two different industries who were looking for a path to expand and extend their impact. It is not uncommon to achieve success in the business world and desire more. I call it moving from success to significance.

At Walmart, our leaders were expected to be involved in their community. We have a strategic Community Giving framework developed by an internal executive advisory council. The council creates a prioritization for the pillars that Walmart will support. At the same time, the Walmart Foundation reviews that strategy to determine where its philanthropic dollars are best invested to complement and support impact. Each executive is encouraged to be an advocate or a sponsor for a cause of his or her choice, one that aligns with this strategic framework. Under each pillar, there are signature nonprofit organizations that can benefit through board service by a current, active Walmart/Sam's Club executive.

Relationships are developed by being open to suggestions with like-minded leaders from many corporations. A leader will gladly support a unique cause, as long as it aligns with their personal, and company, values and strategy. This in itself is a wonderful attribute of servant leadership.

That's how I got involved with Children's Miracle Network Hospitals, where I had the honor to serve on the Board of Governors for sixteen years. I realized firsthand the joy of giving back and the importance of strong leaders working with strong nonprofit organizations. It really is far greater to give than to receive. I've found that servant leadership is rewarded in more ways than monetarily. I was asked to consider joining the Children's Miracle Network Hospital (CMNH) Board following the service of our vice chairman, Don Soderquist. It was an honor to support Don's tenure and passion for CMNH and for children's health. It was an important board seat since Walmart was a founding corporate sponsor and their largest fund-raising partner. But I did not understand the significance of the role for several years.

For close to sixteen years, I had perfect attendance at the bi-annual board meetings. I felt it was my honor and duty to represent the associates and communities that accomplished outstanding fund-raising success. I felt my role was to ask questions for understanding and to be informed as we voted for initiatives and budgets to support strategic growth. But truly my role was to do so much more!

I realized that my role also required developing an understanding about CMNH inside the company. I had a role to inspire our stores, clubs, DCs and their associates to engage in ways that mattered with their local children's hospital. When I realized that I had a two-way responsibility, I began to connect with our associates and hear why they were so passionate about their children's hospital. I visited our facilities to celebrate with the top fund-raisers, and I created challenges with operations-leadership support to increase fund-raising through competitions and recognition. Our people truly amazed us! We took our annual fund-raising from $15M to $22M to $40M and more! These remarkable results were accomplished by passionate associates, customers and members committed to making a difference for the children and the families in their communities. I served as a catalyst, but together we achieved significance.

I discovered that I had the time and the capacity to give to important causes in my life. I found two regional nonprofits to give of my time and talents; one was Northwest Arkansas Community College, and the other was the Jones Center for Families. I began to build a reputation in Northwest Arkansas of service and leadership in the community, and it evolved to deciding how much time I truly could commit to the community and what causes were authentic passions of mine. Make sure that when you serve, you're serving for the right reasons!

I was asked to serve on many local and regional nonprofit boards. I had to narrow them down to three organizations at any one time—one regional, one state-level, and one national. I had to learn how to say no and recommend others as possible leadership choices.

One of my best recommendations was the time when I connected Karen Stuckey, the SVP of Private Brands for Home and Apparel, with the local Boys and Girls Club organization.

Karen had joined Walmart U.S. a few years earlier, and she was ready to get connected in the local community. She had served on several large boards in North Carolina, and it was time for her to find the right organizations to begin her community service in Arkansas. I knew a great place that truly needed her leadership.

I had to say no to the Boys and Girls Club because of my other commitments, but I recommended Karen after getting her permission to make a referral. She has made a huge impact, serving as a board member, chairman of the board, and past chairman. She has made me and our community quite proud! As it turns out, it was the perfect assignment and right on target with her desire and skills. The growth, improvement, and impact she has made in Northwest Arkansas will be felt by generations. That is the power of giving back and giving away opportunities to others.

Today, I serve on three regional boards and one state-level board. I made a name for myself at the state and regional level as a strong fund-raiser and as a leader who will challenge the status quo and help organizations achieve excellence in their space. I am an active and a vocal board member. I started that previous statement with "active," then "vocal." I roll up my sleeves, and I volunteer for assignments that will make the organization better. I take my two-way responsibility seriously. I have a reputation of excellence and action.

I have never regretted the time and energy I invested in the community. There are so many special moments I could share.

I have been serving on the Foundation Board for Arkansas Children's Hospital for more than six years. But we were entering into a significant capital campaign to build a second hospital in the state, located in Springdale, Arkansas. I was asked by the Arkansas Children's Hospital Foundation leadership to serve on the Capital Campaign Strategy Team. I jumped at the opportunity to be part of building a children's hospital! But this was the year I also retired after twenty-six years with Walmart. And the most frequent question I was asked was, "What are you doing now?" My answer was "Helping to build a children's hospital," and the response was always, "Wow! Awesome! How rewarding!" I had a noble and personal answer to that awkward and uncomfortable question—which made a huge difference in my psyche.

So many times, people in the same period of transition respond, "I am still searching," or, "I am taking time to figure that out." Such responses result in a plethora of suggestions and follow-up questions. Having a noble and personal answer makes a huge difference on your self-esteem at a time when you are going through a significant transition. Shortly after I retired, I was given the Athena Woman of the Year Award by the NWA Business Community. I was completely stunned by this honor. My first question was, "Why me?" I never served in the community expecting any recognition or award. The community's response was, "Your answer, 'Why me?' That is why. Because you didn't do it for the recognition."

I served to fill a need and to give back because I have been blessed. However, my actions and impact had not gone unnoticed. I am forever humbled by such a great honor and endorsement that my service matters.

Be known. Start small, pick a cause that is a passion, and then give it your best. If you have more capacity, add another cause of choice. Then do it for the importance of making an impact. Do it with excellence. Do it to develop the skills of servant leadership. Do it for the purpose of bettering the lives of others. Do it for the value it brings to your life.

Do it because it matters.

You will be amazed at how it will mold and define you.

Be Known

1. What are you scattering in life?

2. Do you have your head down or your head up?

3. Are you paying attention to the needs of others or only your own?

4. How are you spending your precious resource of time?

Being known is not an activity of self-promotion. In fact, it is just the opposite.

Being known is about the words others use to describe you. It is also about where you have made a significant impact and others logically connect you and your reputation with potential needs and opportunities to serve.

Chapter 9
MAKING AN IMPACT

"Leadership is not about a title or a destination. It's about impact, influence and inspiration. Impact involves getting results, influence is about spreading the passion you have for your work, and you have to inspire teammates and customers."

—ROBIN S. SHARMA

Life is a series of choices. You can't predict the way everything will go. Assess yourself, and to thine own self be true. That's the rudder you should use to make your decisions on what's right or wrong for you and your family.

Life will throw you numerous unexpected left turns.

What do I mean by that? It means that there are times in your business life, your relationships, your career, or your personal walk that you get a curve ball that you weren't prepared for. It could be a barrier, or it could be an opportunity. Opportunity creates impact, but you have to be flexible enough to step into it and overcome your fear. You can't make an impact unless you see it as an opportunity and lean into the left turn! I remember the opportunity when Joe Hardin, the president of Sam's Club, called me while I was on vacation to offer me an incredible promotion. The new role was completely different than anything I'd done before, but he promised he'd invest in training and support and help me learn and perform well. It was a complete surprise.

I asked him, "Why me?" and he listed all of the leadership qualities he had seen me demonstrate. Then he asked me to think about it. I said, "Yes," even though I was going to enter a position I felt completely unprepared for. The role of confidence is much more important than most people give it credit. With confidence, you can enter into a situation or a job about which you don't have all the knowledge required, depth of experience, or expertise; you can thrive and succeed. If you have confidence you can learn quickly and master the challenge, and if you have confidence in your ability to lead, you will achieve great impact. Wear that confidence as part of your professional suiting. By wearing that confidence, I believed in my capabilities and knew I could learn quickly and succeed.

Sometimes the left turn is that you're fired or that you're released from your role during a restructuring. That can be an unexpected left turn that you have to adapt to without sabotaging yourself, doubting your ability, or demolishing your self-esteem. People will watch you as you respond to your new reality and lead yourself through very tough situations. The challenges may be very personal, but you are being watched and critiqued.

All those in leadership have the opportunity to make an impact on their teams and the individuals that they work with. Your mentoring and feedback could be what pushes someone to greatness. There may be people along the way who become mentors to you—and change your life. They may impact you in ways you've never imagined. Being one of the first women in executive leadership at Walmart, I understood the value of mentoring my team, especially mentoring female leaders across the company. It was my job to see that nothing held them back from success.

I have been in retail for forty years and said yes to many opportunities. There were numerous unexpected left turns that required hard-right decisions. We moved from Omaha, Nebraska, to Des Moines, Iowa, when my company got sold. I made the choice to remain with the new department store when we moved to Iowa. My husband quit his job and moved with me, and he was wildly successful in his career! The move seemed like a fantastic decision. At the same time, the leadership team with my new company did not live up to my expectations, and I did not see an opportunity for growth with the new company after all. Making decisions that are within your comfort zone is where you often get stuck. It wasn't hard to make a decision to move to Iowa and follow my company, because it was part of the growth and evolution of a company I loved. Even though it involved a move, it was still in my comfort zone, and that's often a great limitation for many leaders.

Incredible leadership moments happen at all levels in any organization. Walmart's first female executive vice president of operations was Pat Curran. She had worked her way up in the organization, starting as an hourly associate in the pet department to executive vice president of operations reporting to the president of the Walmart U.S. division. As the EVP, she was responsible for leading and inspiring 1.4 million associates in Walmart U.S. She had earned the opportunity to lead in this new role. But she knew that she would have to lead in a more strategic manner. She reached out for help from me as she prepared to address her team at the Year Beginning Meeting. I was serving in the role of SVP of Change Management and Associate Communications at Walmart U.S. She came to me, when she was about to give her first big speech to 10,000 store operations leaders.

This was going to be her first presentation from the "main stage," and she wanted to stand in front of 10,000 people and inspire them. Her role was to lead them through a transformative change in their roles and changes in how we operated the stores.

I asked her, "How do you want to show up when you address your field leadership team?"

This would be a pivotal opportunity for her; what tone and expectations did she want to set? "How are you going to motivate them to move the business forward? How are you going to rally them? What were the most critical messages to share, and what was the best way to make these points memorable?" These were the kinds of questions she had to be prepared to answer; others were jumping at the chance to hear from her and live up to her expectations. Ask yourself the questions that people might ask you: this is an important component of servant leadership—being intentional and prepared to answer those defining questions.

Once she knew the key components of her message, it was about taking the time to put her message on paper, then bring it to life on stage. I encouraged her to make her message simple and focused so that it would inspire millions. The message would be shared broadly, would enlist support from her direct reports, and would cascade to all associates in 4,000 stores.

This was a defining moment in her leadership. Being able to reach out and ask for help can make or break how you lead. When you need help, do you reach out?

Through this clarity about who she was and how she was going to lead and engage, she took her leadership to a new level. She created a lasting mark of caring, and she taught the associates to see the potential within themselves. Pat's connection with the people and her own personal story inspired the best in our associates and gave them encouragement during a time of change. Even though she moved on to pursue a very different career several years later, the legacy she left behind has been indelible.

As a leader, you have many opportunities throughout your life and career to invest your time in people who show you the potential to do great things. You do that through discernment. As a leader, you must recognize when someone has a special talent or when someone no longer fits a position.

When I took over the Talent Development Team at Walmart U.S., Amanda Griffin became one of the leaders who reported directly to me. She is an amazing talent, who joined our company straight out of college. She started her career being responsible for our MBA recruiting. She was later promoted into the Talent Development Team, where she was responsible for creating training content and delivering tools which prepare associates to do their jobs in the stores. She struggled with how to do her job well and add value because the job required a different set of skills from her previous position. She was faced with developing Compliance Training content, how to report compliance issues, and making sure that she was instilling values on how to do things the right way—always.

After she came to me for advice, I suggested that she go out into the stores and walk in the shoes of the associates she was trying to teach. Once she learned firsthand the struggles of the software and tools that our associates were required to use, she found her voice. When she started to advocate for the associates in the stores, she found her personal inspiration and impact. It was then that she developed a reputation for improving the tools available to our associates and understanding her audience, our front-line associates. She became known as a warrior for our associates. Through this challenge, she began to earn the respect of her peers, her leaders, and herself. I watched her personal transformation, and it was impressive.

As a leader, you have the responsibility of coaching your team or employees to be leaders who truly serve. When you invest in your leaders and make yourself available to them and challenge them to live up to their full potential, you will see similar transformations. Remember that you will change the way they see leadership. They will rise up to your expectations and become advocates for the people they serve.

Since then, Amanda has taken on more complex roles and delivered real solutions, companywide, that simplified the work at store level and delivered efficiency in how work gets done. I invested time in her when she needed it, and she has grown to be an incredible leader. It really is as simple as investing the time to teach and lead.

As a leader, I learned that, sometimes, there are things you never accomplish. You have to be able to see this as a learning for you and move forward. When I was unable to move a big idea from concept to implementation, I would always look in the mirror and assess what I could have done differently. Sometimes, the idea was too early for its time. And sometimes, I made it more difficult than it needed to be. Simplification became an important differentiator for me later in my career. Simplification is quite hard. You have to know the concept inside and out. And then you need to step back from the details and boil the concept down into its simplest form. This takes additional time. But when you can master making something simple and compelling, you can become a person of influence and impact.

Another lesson for me was speaking in sound bites. I had a bad habit of droning on and on. I fell prey to believing that more was better. In fact, the opposite is true. Less is more—because it forces you to identify what is most important in your message and take out the rest. These lessons came after lots of great ideas that never took root. And they came with serious reflection on how I could earn the reputation of being an impact player.

When you are a leader, there will be times when people don't want to hear what you have to say. Their reasons may be based on gender or race, reputation or bias. Or perhaps they just don't like you because of their own insecurities or reasons. You have to discover your path to push through. You have to engage the leaders around you and find a way for your voice to be heard. When people didn't want to hear what I had to say, I felt excluded, but I addressed their wish not to hear me in one-on-one discussions with mentors and trusted leaders. I developed ways to use my voice and be heard. Persuasion through inclusion: that is how I was able to impact positive change.

Had I not felt the responsibility to bring other leaders along, especially women, on my journey, I would not have been able to be part of the evolution for women at Walmart and Sam's Club. If visionary men had not stepped in to include women and diverse leaders at the decision-making table, our company would not have become a great place to work for *all*. This is a legacy I am most proud to have helped create. This is a leadership style that has defined my personal brand and honed my ability to lift others up and help them achieve more than they ever thought possible.

No one gets to the top alone. It takes a team. Understand the value of your team, and you will see them contribute in ways you could never accomplish on your own. If you're not surrounded by the right team, change that right away! Make it your first and most important responsibility to be surrounded by great talent.

Become an Exporter of Talent

What does that mean? Be on the constant lookout for great talent; invest in talented people's development; encourage them to take on tough challenges and growth assignments. Be sure to have talent in the pipeline whom you can promote and grow to fill back the pipeline. Then do it all over again. This will be the most important legacy you can leave. Instead of being known as an importer of talent, become known for identifying great talent and preparing talented people for bigger roles and contributions. Importers of talent are leaders that do not invest in the personal growth of their teams. They expect other leaders to develop great talent. They choose from other teams the people they want to promote. But they never fill positions with up-and-coming talent from their own teams.

As leaders, we have a responsibility to recognize and respect our employees and our teams, and to surround ourselves with the very best talent. We all have the responsibility to groom future leaders, bringing them along as they excel and succeed.

This chapter is about making an impact. That requires leaders to be great developers of talent and to learn how you maximize every opportunity to make an impact at work. It comes down to leadership and understanding how to champion ideas and build trust.

Techniques You Can Use

Step 1: Be clear about the expected outcome.

Use data and models to describe the current situation. Involve others to envision what is possible and why it matters.

Step 2: Be memorable.

Use stories and examples that can be remembered when you define the impact that you want to deliver.

Step 3: Celebrate the small wins.

Give people hope, and recognize progress. Show them how this new result will be of benefit to them.

Step 4: Communicate like water on stone.

Be consistent and constant. Use every opportunity to reinforce the goal.

Step 5: Do not settle.

Never settle for anything less than exceeding the expectations you and your team defined.

Exercise: Pick one area in your life where you are trying to drive for results and leave a lasting impact. Then create a plan, using the five steps above.

Watch how you will transform the results you deliver and how you lead by influence.

Chapter 10
BE A VISIONARY

"Keep your eyes on the stars,
and your feet on the ground."

—THEODORE ROOSEVELT

Inspire a shared vision. If you create a vision, rally and show others how your vision can positively impact them, helping them find personal growth and purpose in their work. Not everyone is a natural visionary; you may be the strongest one in the room. Visionaries often lead change. The good news is that you can inspire and lead others to enable your vision, even though it may take a lot of communication to get everyone on board.

You don't have to be the sole inspiration in the room. Not everyone will understand your vision, but odds are one person out of a hundred in that room will understand it. Be a visionary "lifeline" to that one person. If you're the leader of a team and need to get everyone on board to execute your vision or a new corporate initiative, your social equity will go a long way. Be a high-integrity leader that builds trust through communication. It's much easier to communicate a vision when people trust you.

I recently spoke on a panel at John Brown University with business graduate students. The question I was given centered on the most impactful leadership readings I would recommend and the effect it had on my leadership. The first book I referenced was *The Leadership Challenge* by James Kouzes and Barry Z. Posner. They developed a leadership model on the basis of years of research, and it was one of the first books written on successful leadership traits. From the Foreword by Tom Peters: "Leaders thrive on change; exercise 'control' by means of a worthy and inspiring vision of what might be, arrived at jointly with their people; and understand that empowering people by expanding their authority, rather than standardizing them by shrinking their authority, is the only course to sustained relevance and vitality."

This book was first published in 1987. At that time, there were very few books written about leadership, and

I was a young leader, rising quickly through the ranks in my company. It seemed as if every eighteen months I was being promoted and given more responsibility. To top it off, I was a young woman leading a team of primarily men, and I had to be credible and earn their trust. This book, with its proven leadership model that could be replicated and measured, was a beacon of light for me when I was defining, teaching, and reinforcing great leadership skills.

Leadership Is in the Eye of the Follower

When a leader is asked to lead a new team or function, the early work required of an exemplary leader is to develop a forward focused vision that captures the hearts and dreams of the people on the team. As a young leader, I had to capture the people's imagination, their hopes and aspirations. I had to move the conversation past competence to aspiration. And I had to ensure that the vision was simple, relevant, worthy, and aligned to a higher calling. I began to master this practice as I evolved in my leadership journey. In the roles where I struggled, after much reflection, I can now say that I was deficient in this practice. I did not see the bigger picture of where we were going and what the future could look like for us all. And if I did not see it, I could not communicate it and inspire others to come along on the journey.

In roles where I mastered this practice, I could pull a team out of despair and potential ruin to a place where they were valued and where they understood their purpose and inspired work performance that they never knew was in them.

It is in this reflection that I discovered the critical importance of being a visionary.

Bring Others Along

Reaching across and into the organization is an important differentiator of servant leaders. And that has been especially true for women.

Former Secretary of State Madeline Albright has been famously quoted: "There is a special place in hell for women who do not help other women." The 1990s was the era in which I was being groomed as a young leader. I had observed women leaders who behaved like Ms. Albright's hell-doomed women along my journey. Why did this exist? Because there were so few women in senior leadership roles and they were threatened by other women. It was as if their gender had gotten them into their positions of leadership! If that was all that had gotten them there, they were shortchanging their talents, their hard work, and their qualifications. What a shame!

I was never a leader who did not believe in bringing other women along. It just wasn't in me to be competitive with other women. I wanted to help them, and I still do today.

I knew that women, as well as men, helped groom me and prepare me for growth and expanded responsibility. I had been a student of leadership, and I believe in the power of talent. When I see talent, determination, and vision, I want to extend women, and men, a rope of support and future opportunities. Be available for mentorship, and lead by example while following, listening, and being open to feedback, as well. In order to be gracious and strong, you're going to need to allow people to make their own mistakes. Extend the rope, and be the one they know they can go to for feedback and development. Add value to every relationship around you.

The day I was promoted to the first female EVP at Walart Inc. was, of course, monumental for me! I broke through the glass ceiling. It wasn't luck. I had worked hard and earned the promotion. I had to prove I was right for the job by stepping up to every challenge, by not giving up, and by meeting every test head-on. But I did have some amazing mentors along the way who invested in my success. Finding those people is entirely up to you. If you don't have them, don't sit on the sidelines like a wallflower and feel sorry for yourself. You need to seek out people who will help you elevate and rise in your leadership walk. Get clarity about what you want and what is possible. Then reach out to seek mentors to guide you on your journey.

For eight years at Sam's Club, I showed up and proved that I was both qualified and prepared. On the day my promotion was announced, the auditorium of people stood and applauded. It happened during a highly public Saturday morning meeting all management associates were required to attend. Before the applause came to an end, Lee Scott said, "And now what are you going to do for the other women across the company?"

I turned my head quickly from the audience to Lee Scott and responded, "I will bring them along!" And there it began—a purpose bigger than me—and one that has defined my future. Lee was making a point to me and to all the leaders in the room. This was a breakthrough moment, and with it came a responsibility and a commitment to do more.

This achievement is something that can never be taken away from me—it is a moment in my career that I worked hard to achieve. Aside from the promotion, I had conquered fear, put aside doubt, and believed in myself. Believing in yourself is a key principle. Whether it is a promotion or an unexpected left turn, the key attribute to stepping up to a challenge unknown is courage and belief that you can do it.

Imagine the Possible

In the early stages of my career, I was not known as a visionary. I saw the limitations of budgets, talent, and circumstances. But the real limitation was me. I concentrated on being a rule follower and living up to the guidelines that were given to me for expected performance. I was the one on the team who brought definition and structure to a vision created by others. It was after being passed over for a few promotions and hearing, "You are not quite ready," that I realized the importance of being a visionary if I wanted to grow beyond my current level.

I saw that the people getting promoted had a unique skill to imagine the possible. They invested time in thinking beyond what was incremental; they spent time studying best-in-class solutions; they tested ideas to take what they discovered and made the ideas better. And then they spent time gathering other smart people to test out their ideas and improve their ideas beyond their original vision.

One of my early successes with being a visionary happened at Pace Membership Warehouse. I was the senior vice president of Human Resources, and we were in the club business. We were competing against Price Club, who had invented the warehouse club channel, and Sam's Club, who had honed the club business and was growing rapidly in our markets. We had to create our points of differentiation, and customer service was what we chose. We studied the competition, and we studied other retailers. We built a low-cost, high-value customer-service model that allowed us to differentiate our clubs. A brilliant woman by the name of Soraya Cartwright was on my team. We built this strategy and developed the tools and the methodology for implementation, and we gained the support and funding from the executive leadership team. We created a different experience for our members. We were able to inspire our employees to deliver excellence through personal customer service that differentiated us from our competitors. And we instilled a pride for working at Pace Membership Warehouse that allowed us to grow. We created a sense of pride that even union-organizing attempts could not diminish.

The power of being a visionary became a part of my reputation as a leader. And when I reflect on the roles and the moments in my career where I did not live up to my own expectations or potential, they all happened at times when I did not have a clear and inspiring vision.

Critical Job Skills for the Future

The pace of change in today's workplace is unprecedented. The skills needed to be successful are very different today, because they are based on disruptive technology. Digital competencies will be the foundation upon which the job skills of the future are based. As I visit classrooms and consult with education innovators, it is becoming clear that technological know-how will not be enough to compete effectively. To be successful in this rapidly changing workplace, skills like creativity and collaboration will be required to navigate career and industry shifts.

I have been investing quite a bit of time to research and understand the skills that will be necessary for the workforce of the future. McKinsey's Global Chief Learning Officer Nick van Dam has just published a new book entitled *Humility Is the New Smart: Rethinking Human Excellence in the Smart Machine Age*. He has identified the top ten skills that will be in demand in the near future. The top three are complex problem solving, critical thinking, and creativity. I reference this research because I see these skills as requirements to becoming a visionary leader. An observation made by a visionary college dean is that a master's in fine arts will be the critical degree for future CEOs. The traditional business or marketing degrees do not master the skill of creative thinking that will be required in the near future.

Being a visionary also means being a lifelong learner. Investing in yourself to remain relevant was a personal discovery I made when I realized that the great strategic leaders in my industry were constant learners. In today's business environment, strategy can no longer be left to a few visionary leaders at the top of the organization. The ability to see what is possible and to put ideas together that solve problems and the ability to formulate a path to achieve your vision are all critical capabilities of a visionary leader.

And a visionary leader turns his or her vision into reality by creating a vivid image of the future. Putting your vision on paper and representing it in a diagram or simple model takes time and a deep understanding of the details or critical components of your vision. I did not understand the power of a simple model or a diagram until I was asked to lead large-scale change in the business. One example occurred when we implemented the very first membership-fee increase at Sam's Club. It required creating a compelling case for our members. We had to give them reasons and benefits for renewing at a slightly higher fee. We had to explain the increase through letters, online messaging, marketing brochures, and scripts for our associates to encourage and reinforce what would be better for our members. We created a simple model that we called, "Better, Better, Better." And we built a comprehensive strategy to provide better prices on merchandise, to add better member benefits to the card, and to deliver a better member experience when members shopped in our clubs. The model was simple; it clearly articulated every department's role in this strategy; and it was easy to remember and inspired our associates to deliver on our promise to our members. I never forgot that example. I began to use the concept of a simple model, compelling to the people who were targets of the change and inspiring the team to be part of a better future after the changes were successfully implemented.

When you are given a leadership role, you must quickly envision a new sense of purpose for your area of responsibility. And once you create your vision, the next steps are to rally the team and inspire them—to enlist them by appealing to their values, hopes, and dreams. Will it solve the need that the business has asked you to solve? What is it the company needs in the next couple of months? Years? Look at a company's course down the road and identify early wins that can be accomplished in the present.

The very best solutions come when you flip the problem upside down, move it around, and then do something bold. Think of the Einstein quotation your high school English teacher might have told you: **"Insanity is doing the same thing over and over again and expecting different results."**

If we keep using the same method to solve a problem, a solution will never come! Experiment with problem solving and with studying the strategies of others. Creating a vision means listening and learning. Form a bond with your team, and enlist them to join you as agents of change.

Being a visionary begins with inspiring a shared vision, selling that vision internally, celebrating successes, examining failures, and moving that vision forward to impact success.

Sharing Your Vision

During my tenure at Walmart U.S., I worked for an incredible female leader, Gisel Ruiz. She was the COO, and I led the Talent Development and Talent Management functions which were support teams for the U.S. business. On this day, I presented the new vision we had developed for the Talent Development Team. Gisel was impressed and then asked me a leadership-changing question: "If I walked onto the floor where your people work, would they be able to tell me why their job exists? Could they share your mission and vision and how it impacts them?"

You can talk about your mission and vision, but if you never put it on paper, how is it going to make an impact? How will your team understand what they are working for and towards? If you aren't teaching it in every leadership meeting and reinforcing it when you bring in new associates, then you will miss the mark. You must be consistently reinforcing your mission and vision, through the celebration of small and large wins, to the storytelling by individuals about how they made a personal difference.

My answer to Gisel was, "They may not today, but they will tomorrow." You see, it struck me that I had not written my mission and vision down. And I certainly had not communicated them often. But I could change that immediately!

It became clear to me that I needed to put our vision on paper, in the form of a one-page diagram. I needed to share it, at every chance I had to enlist, reinforce, and celebrate it as a mantra for our team. This was one of the most profound lessons I have applied inside a corporation or a nonprofit organization. If your team cannot share the vision with you and use it as a measuring stick for their performance, then you have missed the mark of a strong, exemplary leader.

I worked with my four senior leaders, and we created the first of many one-page visual documents representing the vision, the mission, the purpose, and the goals for Walmart U.S. Talent Development. We gave all team members a copy. We laminated copies and asked them to hang them in their offices or cubicles. We talked about them at every All Hands meeting, and we committed to cover them with every new associate on our team. When Gisel tested if we had clarity and alignment, we passed with pride and ownership.

This lesson has been extremely helpful in business and in my nonprofit board roles. If you have a team or an organization you lead, invest in the time to create your one pager to inform, engage, and inspire your team. It makes a difference!

Certain events are a turning point in your life. When I broke my ankle, I was practically immobile. And then depression followed. That accident was a turning point in my life and one that caused my mind to move when my body couldn't. Creating this book pulled me out of that dark cloud. My mission was to write, and my vision was to inspire change. Sometimes a tragedy or problem can jumpstart your vision. When facing adversity of any kind, you have a hard-right decision to make. You have been dealt an unexpected left turn. How will you handle it?

Don't ever forget to dream and reflect on your long-term life plan. Whatever it is you're facing is just a setback to that original plan. How do you overcome this setback and use it to propel you to a new, and better, outcome? In that dilemma is a powerful response.

Visionary Leadership

What are the Characteristics of a Visionary Leader?

- Able to see around corners and act like a headlight to illuminate the road ahead.

- Inspire others to come along on the journey.

- Define a vision for the future, but do not limit how each team member can contribute.

- Describe the future in a confident and enthusiastic way.

What type of leader are you?

Visionary leadership is important when you are in the midst of change or transformation.

Chapter 11

DEFINE YOUR BRIGHT LINES

"Effective people lead their lives and manage their relationships around principles; ineffective people attempt to manage their time around priorities and their tasks around goals. Think effectiveness with people; efficiency with things."

—STEVEN COVEY

What are bright lines?

If you're in a situation that completely throws you off, start with having a clear understanding of the personal values you hold dear. Like traveling on a highway, it's important to stay in your lane—not crossing the bright-yellow lines.

Take a step back and look at the situation with a neutral mentality. What will you stand for?

What are the things that deeply motivate you and inspire you to do your best work? What are your nonnegotiables?

Taking time to evaluate and define your central core values and beliefs will position you for success as you navigate unexpected left turns.

It's also important to note that Bright Lines are not just about having core values - they're the ability to actively see a pattern before anyone else and act accordingly. These values are not just reserved for the C-suite, but for leaders of all experience levels. And, they're crucial for making the hard-right decisions that help you succeed.

I've seen how a lack of courage can threaten any organization. And I've learned that these downward spirals boil down to two things: incremental tolerance and leadership by omission.

In incremental tolerance, leaders turn their heads and accept gray-area behavior from those around them. They often find themselves saying, "Just this time" or, "It's not really against the rules" or, "It might be fuzzy, but it's OK." This behavior does not always stem from bad intentions, but it can cause irreparable damage over time.

In leadership by omission, leaders make a conscious decision to remove themselves from a situation that requires strong advocacy. They may say, "This isn't really a problem in our organization" or, "I don't really need to be the one to advocate on this issue" or "I'd rather not stir the pot, even though I know it is the right thing to do." They will then remove themselves from the situation by leaving a job or role or by simply doing nothing at all.

These two shortcomings serve as immediate red flags that we as leaders must be cognizant of to ensure organizational success. These shortcomings are not just a C-suite issue; they are relevant at any level.

All leaders will come to a point in their career, whether they are entrepreneurs or CEOs, where they have to fire someone. Perhaps the firing comes from a performance issue, or maybe there are major layoffs coming. Regardless of the why, sometimes you can be faced with making the decision to remove employees that no longer fit their jobs, or their roles have been eliminated in your company.

The decision to fire someone, to remove that person from your organization, isn't a normal everyday decision that you make on the fly. In every instance over my career at different organizations, I always went above and beyond to research and investigate any and all instances where I would be responsible for letting someone go.

One instance happened when I hired a brilliant woman who had a skill set I did not possess that the club business really needed. She had created a simple but highly relevant member strategy. We were becoming more relevant and important to our members, and her strategy was very successful. She was incredibly productive and worked for me for about two years. She was a highly valued asset at Sam's Club, and while I was focused on her skills and the strategy she had developed, I did not see how she was treating the team. Eventually I learned that she had demanded so much from her team, that she would often talk down to them in front of other associates and really made them feel marginalized because they didn't have her skill set.

Her team was full of good people and hard workers. If she had brought them along with her, helped them grow as she excelled, many would have executed with excellence for her and the company.

In any company or business, when someone is delivering results that are critically needed, he or she seems invaluable, and it may be hard to see any negatives that are tagging along with that success. I was starving for the right mix of technical strategy and consumer skills that would supplement my ability to sell it inside the organization. I had blinders on and did not see how she was treating the team. It took the team to share the problem with the vice chairman of Walmart Inc. When the problem was brought to my attention, I learned much more about what was happening. I had to make the tough judgement call. Despite her brilliant skills and strong strategy, I had to ensure that my associates were being treated with dignity and respect.

Why was it important to side with my associates? We had to make sure they knew that success wasn't just about results.

This is a tough issue that most leaders will face. The toughest call to make happens when someone is excelling in their role but they are failing their team. When you make that hard-right decision, you are sending the message that results are *not* more important than how you achieve them.

Leaders often let it go too far. I did. Many leaders will ignore the problem, hoping that it will just go away. What if your company critically needs the skills of persons who do not fit the company culture? What if their leadership style is completely opposite of what you preach and teach?

It took me two years to repair my relationships with the associates on the team, all because I had turned a blind eye. I had sent the message that results were more important than respect for our people. The line drawn in this story became crystal clear. If you are delivering results and excelling at the expense of your integrity, that isn't success.

What do you do when the line isn't so clearly drawn? As someone in leadership, you will make choices that are based on a gray area rather than black-and-white. When you have a gray area, you face into it, examine the facts with respect to everyone, and make your decision with integrity.

There was a time when I had to let a gentleman go who was well-respected and admired within the company. He had an incredible background of organizations in which he'd worked. However, we learned a year and a half into his tenure that not all of his credentials may have been factual. That was enough to raise a red flag and initiate a close evaluation of his leadership behaviors and ethics. During the investigation, a sexual harassment allegation was also brought forward. We take harassment of any kind very seriously. It eventually came down to his word versus the individual who had made the claim, and I had to take swift action. We came to the agreement that this was not the right company for him. The quicker you can address the challenge, the clearer you set the standard for other team members.

Leaders must have the courage to address unacceptable behavior and make the hard-right decisions. You can't coach people to excellence if integrity and respect do not exist.

In any leadership role, whether it be CEO, entrepreneur, or executive leadership team, you must find the courage to make the tough choices, even in gray areas.

What happens when those terminations are layoffs? How do you select who stays and who goes? Several times, I found myself leading the initiative at Walmart that resulted in layoffs or cost cutting. As a business grows, there can be too much infrastructure in the business. We never made these layoff decisions without facts and a fair and unbiased process.

We established fair and consistent methods, which are still in place today. Even when the process is fair and sound, it does not change that people are being impacted and that we must treat all people with dignity and respect. It always comes down to how an individual leader treats his or her people, especially during times of crisis and despair. In the small actions you take or the large decisions you make, showing care and concern for the people you lead is the defining moment for earning their trust and respect.

Taking a stand isn't always easy, and it requires a special mix of grit and courage that's essential for making a meaningful and virtuous difference. Below are four ways to become a more courageous leader.

1.   Understand your bright lines.

Like traveling a highway, it's important to stay in your lane of virtue—not crossing the bright-yellow lines that influence your decision making. Take a step back and look at the situation with intentionality: what will you stand for? What will you not tolerate? What are the things that really motivate and inspire you to lead well? What are your nonnegotiables? Taking time to evaluate yourself and define your very core will position you for success as you navigate unexpected challenges.

2.   Ask the right questions.

Asking the right questions is essential for spotting courageous opportunities.

These questions include the following:

Have you avoided calling out behavior that's unacceptable?

Are there situations where you say, "I'll just let this go by"?

Is it unclear to you or your team where you stand on a particular topic?

Would people on your team expect you to have a point of view on a situation?

Would people on your team expect you to answer to a particular scenario?

If your answer is, "No," to the last two questions, you may have a blind spot in a certain area and may need to consider requesting trustworthy feedback from others.

3. Speak up.

When you see something, say something. We tell this to our kids when it comes to school bullying, yet why does it stop there? Often we think we outgrow these principles, thinking that it is not our responsibility to take a stand for what's right or that we will kill our career for doing so. However, a willingness to stand up, to demonstrate bravery, and to withstand the tests of tension that come with courageous leadership will give you a true sense of purpose as you navigate your leadership journey. Having courage as a leader doesn't mean acting disrespectfully or recklessly. Be self-aware and identify the best approach to take on an issue without any ill behavior.

4. Model the way.

Use this opportunity to demonstrate what it looks like to lead with courage. Now more than ever, we need courageous leaders in our business and in our country. Whether you're a CEO facing the front lines of leadership or an intern just getting their feet wet, your actions have a ripple effect on those around you. And when you shift your way of thinking, you will realize where you are is not about you, but about helping others rise to success.

It's all about respect and integrity.

In all my years of leadership, the four values that I value most—respect, excellence, service, and integrity—have only grown stronger. My commitment to be a leader who brings others along, as well as a leader that provides them a safety net, was and still is important. It mattered to me and the people I served to create a place where my team could work with dignity and respect, and then to reward them with an environment where they could flourish. That is when you change as a leader, from someone who wants to be the best in their space to someone who wants to see everyone else be the best. Not only will your life change as a leader, but the lives of everyone you interact with will change as well.

Bright Lines

1. Understand your bright lines. They may not be top of mind. Spend time digging deep to define what you will stand for and what you will not.

2. Ask the right questions. This is critical to spotting courageous opportunities. Have you avoided calling out unacceptable behavior? Are there situations where you say, "I'll just let this go by"?

3. Speak up. Is there a situation you recall where you saw something and you should have said something? What were the reasons why you did not speak up?

4. Model the way. Your actions have a ripple effect. What will it take for you to be willing to demonstrate courage?

Courageous leadership can be lonely and gut-wrenching. After all, having the courage to do what is right even if it's going to have a negative consequence on you is easier said than done. But when you exercise the discipline of courage, you will truly know what you are made of as a leader, and others will experience the joy that comes from your bravery.

Chapter 12
THE SECRET INGREDIENT: RESILIENCE

"Life doesn't get easier or more forgiving, we get stronger and more resilient."

—STEVE MARABOLI

Have you ever walked out of a meeting and said to yourself, "I am better than that"?

Have you left a meeting, licking your wounds and saying, "Where did that come from?"

Have you ever walked away from a meeting, asking, "What did I do to deserve that?" It has happened to us all. If you've ever worked in a corporate setting, you've been exposed to a wide variety of leadership styles, opinions, and possibly even criticism.

I once worked for a CEO who treated people harshly in front of others just for sport. He wanted to see what you were made of. He thought he was developing you to know your business better than anyone else.

Have you ever had a CEO turn to you in the middle of a heated debate about strategy and publicly disagree with the core elements of your direction, in front of everyone? I was so mad I had to go outside, take a walk to let off steam and get away, so I did not respond out of emotion.

Week after week, have you ever attended a corporate leadership meeting and been ridiculed in front of 300 fellow officers? And at the end of the meeting, have you stood up to greet a line of supporters and "friends" to console you, to give you a pep talk on how well you handled that interrogation, or to make suggestions on how to prepare for next week? Have you ever been called to the trash cans outside the building after a key leader meeting and been challenged as to whether you were on the team or off the team? By the vice chairman of the company?

I have experienced each of these situations and I could go on and on, but you get the point. Sometimes corporate America may feel like high school again. It's important to be a leader, and it's important to fit in, if only to get along with your authority figures, but it's also important not to lose who you are. You've got to stay gracious and strong and open to learning. And, sometimes, receive criticism, whether it's warranted or not. Life and work are full of adversity, and it's the way you manage life and work that defines you as a leader.

If you have experienced similar scenarios, your gut is wrenching because they bring back terrible memories and emotions. These are the moments that shape and define you at work. These are the moments for which your bright lines are your compass. These are the moments when you want to fold under the disgrace or disgust. Now is the time when you decide that this will not be the narrative about you, your team, or your work.

It is survival of the fittest! Every day! This is real life in intensely competitive businesses. This is not uncommon in business. In my younger years, I thought this type of leadership was vile and cruel. Why would you subject yourself to this toxic environment? But I had already been swept up to believe in the mission and values of the company. I believed in the culture. This was a special place, and they needed me as much as I wanted to contribute and make an impact. It was the world's largest stage, but it was also the most compassionate and thrilling corporation that challenged me to bring my best to work, *every day*! I drank the Kool-Aid when I joined. I had been groomed and taught by the leaders who built this great company. I knew that we were working for something greater than all of us.

There was a sense of oneness and of mission: our customers and members, our associates, and our stores and clubs. We were taught the importance of serving the stores and clubs. We were taught that the customer and member is number one. We were taught that Walmart Inc. was a family—a very special family. We stood together for a common mission that was noble and important. We had an emotional connection that kept us united as one.

The company and the culture made me better. I had to know my business better than anyone else. If I was asked a fair question, I must know the answer. If I could not defend a direction I had set, then why should anyone support me with resources and trust my strategy?

The Finesse Is in the How

All CEOs taught lessons in their own ways and styles. Their motive was to teach and inspire. Their objective was to apply the lessons of leadership in ways that could be replicated and applied broadly. You felt a sense of urgency to go back to your team and share and teach. It was a culture of oneness and alignment. It was a culture of celebration and inspiration. It was a culture of honor for fighting for the customer and member and being nimble and responsive to their changing needs and demands.

Resilience became the badge of courage to stand up and find the inner strength to rise above. But it required a shift in mind-set to lead from a position of resilience and purpose. I had to ask myself five golden questions:

- How can I rise above the grips of my current situation?
- How can I create opportunity for others when I feel the weight of the world crushing me?
- How can I muster the confidence to lead authentically?
- How can I influence those around me in a positive way?
- And amidst it all, how can I remain gracious and strong?

Resilient leaders find a way to excel in the most challenging situations, and they know that true success comes from not only being your best self but also replicating that behavior in others.

Resilient leaders foster their ability to find the lesson in the situation and use it as an opportunity to reframe where they go from here. They find the inner strength and drive to live up to their full potential. Remaining positive is a key to being resilient leaders, because they know that positivity is a choice.

Resilience

How can you become more resilient?

If you agree that resilience is the secret ingredient, can you develop greater resilience? The answer is yes.

1. Start by thinking back on times when you have been courageous and faced into adversity, trauma, tragedy, threats or significant sources of stress.

    • Describe how you were courageous and persevered. Give yourself credit for how you made it through.

    • Write down the critical behaviors and techniques you deployed.

2. Take on a challenge that will be hard to master but is not emotional or an unexpected left turn.

    • The purpose of this challenge is to practice mastery to help prepare you for future situations that are emotional.

    • Develop a frame of reference to see situations as challenges and not threats.

3. Enlist the help of friends or professionals who you trust and who care.

    • I reached out for grief counseling when my husband passed away.

    • When experiencing a job loss, reach out to your network and to outplacement professionals.

    • Seek out support. Resilient people know that they need help to navigate the unknown path ahead.

4. Take control where you can.

- It may feel like you have no control over your situation. Identify what you do have control over and then exercise your control and build a plan to fall forward through small actions and decisions each day.

- Develop a mental model to fight back and resist letting the situation defeat your inner spirit. You are in control of your outlook and behavior. Check in with yourself to be sure that the situation does not define you.

5. Leverage the lessons that are all around you to grow beyond the boundaries of the situation and become a beacon of hope and inspiration.

There is no doubt that resilient leaders feel a strong sense of gratitude and satisfaction that only comes from true grit and discipline. After resilient leaders are tested and thriving, resilience becomes the badge of honor and the reward for staying the course.

Chapter 13

NAVIGATING TRANSITIONS

"Times of transition are strenuous, but I love them. They are an opportunity to purge, rethink priorities, and be intentional about new habits. We can make our new normal any way we want it."

—KRISTIN ARMSTRONG

I have come to learn that life is filled with transitions and that how we navigate them is an art.

This chapter is dedicated to honing your ability to navigate transitions with grace and purpose. When I say transitions, I mean entry into the workforce, reentry into the workforce, loss of a loved one, loss of a job, or even retirement, as well as new and unexpected left turns that propel you into rewarding next chapters of life, such as marriage, parenting, relocation, career breakthroughs, and personal breakthroughs.

Research conducted by Network of Executive Women (NEW) defines a transition as "a significant shift in personal or professional circumstances that impacts how leaders interact at work and meaningfully alters their circles of both influence and support." In my experience, this also applies to transitions outside the workplace.

I often refer to these moments as "transitioning to next."

The art is in defining who you are at your core, staying true to your authentic self throughout the journey, falling forward when you are not in control of the circumstances, and navigating daily with a belief in yourself and a remarkable future ahead. Being open to embrace the positive opportunities that may come your way is just as important as preparing yourself for how you are going to handle negative challenges. Everything in life is a choice, which is why it is important to find the way to face into each transition and be open to saying yes to new opportunities you discover on the other side.

One of the most roller-coaster life transitions I have tackled is leaving a career I loved!

A career defined me and that made me feel happy and fulfilled in order to discover what was possible and remarkable in my next chapter of life. Life is about challenging yourself, and that was a challenge! There are so many ups and downs that include: emotional preparedness, as well as financial and lifestyle preparedness. Research published by Ameriprise Financial, Age Wave and Harris Interactive, based on The New Retirement Mindscape Study, uncovered five distinct and predictable stages of retirement.

Stage 1

Imagination: People have high expectations of adventure and empowerment.

Stage 2

Anticipation: People have high expectations about achieving their dreams, mixed with increasing anxiety about readiness, financially and emotionally.

Stage 3

Liberation: People have an experience of great excitement, relief, and enthusiasm.

Stage 4

Reorientation: People have an emotional-letdown period, where four distinct profiles emerge: Empowered Reinventors (19 percent), Carefree Contents (19 percent), Uncertain Searchers (22 percent), and Worried Strugglers (40 percent).

Stage 5

Reconciliation: People have increased contentment, acceptance, and personal reflection.

While this research is specific to a retirement mind-set, I think it well describes the stages for many of life's unexpected left turns. For illustrative purposes, let's use what I call "the transitioning to next" for retirement as our practical application.

Key insights for me have been the following:

How you leave, how you choose to be recognized, or if you just walk away are all choices you make. Don't give away this opportunity to others; realize that your exit is a direct reflection of *you*. And it can be navigated and influenced to speak volumes about your character.

One of the most frequent coaching situations I encounter today is how to navigate a gracious exit amidst a tumultuous situation. It is a highly emotional time for anyone. It takes courage. And it requires strength and confidence to state what you need and how your exit will be positioned.

1. Be sure you are leaving on good terms. Even if there is a negative "story" around your circumstances, how you choose to show up and behave says everything about your character.

2. Use your voice to share what you would like to accomplish during your exit. Do not leave your wishes unstated. Be realistic, but ask. If you leave it to others, you will most likely be disappointed. This is *your* exit; manage it as you have managed and navigated your career.

3. Influence every detail. What will be said about why you are leaving? Where will this information be shared, and by whom? When will this information be shared? If there is a written announcement, ask to read it and edit it before it is distributed. Be sure it reflects the leader you want to leave as your legacy.

4. Be prepared with your comments. Think about what you will say in advance of sharing this news with anyone other than your trusted life partner. Do not share the news widely until *you* are ready with your words and actions. You want to manage the narrative.

5. Stay true to your character. Do not drop any balls or leave work unfinished or unassigned. Stay engaged to the end. Respect this decision and respect the people who have supported you and have been a part of your team. Thank them; be kind in every interaction; leave with your character intact and your head held high.

Transitioning well to next is all about preparedness. Have a vision for your last day at work long before it is upon you. Use it as your navigation tool to design your exit strategy. Write down the critical elements in your mind that speak to your character and legacy. Conduct yourself in a way that will make you proud and hold your head up high as you step up to discover a new chapter in your life.

So many women who reach the height of their career are just opting out. *Fortune* magazine published an article highlighting women who have been recognized in the *Fortune* Most Powerful Women over the past ten years, to find out what are they doing now. What is so interesting about this article is that some of these women lost interest and energy to continue the pursuit of that C-suite job. Instead they have opted out; they have chosen to retire or to become an entrepreneur, or they have stepped out of the workforce.

A couple of them are still pushing forward to achieve that C-suite job, but it requires grit and perseverance.

One of the female executive leaders featured in this follow-up story is Pat Curran. Pat is a leader I worked with closely and admire very much. She left her career at Walmart at the age of forty-two and chose not to reenter the workforce right away; instead, she went back to school. She got her nursing degree, and now she is a volunteer nurse.

Why is that important?

Because she knew that nursing had been her calling for her entire life, and now she does it completely free of compensation.

She spent money and time on obtaining her degree, and she was employed at a hospital for a fraction of a second. But she aspired to provide care and service through nursing by creating a different model. It is her calling, and she is exceptional in her field. She created her path by blending the two. Today, she serves by volunteering three days a week. She is an example of a real servant leader. Her measuring stick is not the same as in traditional business metrics. She measures her contribution by truly serving the parents, the staff, and the babies in the hospital. She has chosen to volunteer in the neonatal unit.

On the day I announced my decision to retire, we revealed the news during the Global Officer Meeting. Doug McMillon was the first one in line to shake my hand, and the line to give me a hug and best wishes kept growing in length. The comment I will never forget was one made by a fairly new executive at the company with whom I had worked closely upon joining.

She approached me with tears in her eyes and said, "Did you hear that gasp?! It was remarkable. And they would not sit down! You have earned that respect and adoration after a career well led, and I can only hope to receive a similar expression when I reach the end of my career. Will you help me?"

"Of course," I said.

It's my life goal to help make sure this happens for so many others.

She was not the only one to say "Well done," "Thank you," and to relay so many stories shared about the impact I had made on them throughout my tenure. I could never have imagined a greater moment. But every investment I had made in others came back to me many times over on that day and over the next six weeks. My retirement reception was a wonderful tribute. Many current leaders, past leaders, and associates from across Sam's Club and Walmart filled the Home Office Auditorium. My daughter sat by my side. And I am sure David was present and seated beside me.

Leaders who played important roles in my career stood up to share comments of respect and appreciation. A letter written by Mike Duke, the former CEO of Walmart Inc. was read. Doug McMillon, the current CEO and several members of his direct-report team were present, and the reception included cake, punch, mixed nuts, and mints!

One of the most important gifts I received was a word cloud created by the Women's Officer Caucus and presented to me by the WOC president and very close friend, Karen Stuckey. I have included a copy of this word cloud at the end of the book. It is a cherished item in my home office, on full display for everyone who visits. It is especially meaningful because it is a compilation of all the words that WOC members shared when describing me as a leader. Words that appear in a larger font are the words shared most often; words such as "trailblazer," "advocate," "enthusiastic," "brave," and "culture champion" pop out on the page. And so many more words that make me swell with pride. There is no greater gift than recognition by your peers that express their true respect and appreciation for your impact.

I could never have imagined an exit as gracious as the one I experienced. But I had sown the seeds for a remarkable expression by the character and sacrifices I had made for others along my journey.

I am not finished!

I've set new goals, and I'm excited to discover a future filled with possibilities. I am speaking, coaching, advising, and giving back to many broad and important projects across the region and the country. I am helping to build a new children's hospital in Northwest Arkansas; I am developing human-resource systems and governance policies for nonprofit boards, I am speaking at numerous leadership development conferences and development programs, and I am working in the public education space to bring innovation and strategy to transform high school student preparedness for college and the workplace. The opportunities to make an impact are broad and deep, and I am honored and grateful for the remarkable experiences. I'm living proof that you can reinvent yourself even if you're not sure what that looks like yet.

Transitions

Are you facing a moment of life transition?

If so, how well are you navigating through it?

Here are a few coping skills that I learned to help me navigate successfully through change.

1. Learn to express your feelings and your interests.

2. Build your support system and accept their help.

3. Acknowledge what you are leaving behind. This is the first step to accepting the new.

4. Explore and imagine the new possibilities for your life. Write them down and create a vision for what is exciting and possible.

5. Don't get discouraged. Successful transitions take time.

6. Become an "empowered reinventor" and discover how you can evolve to the next level of happiness and joy.

7. Take daily steps toward your vision.

Transitions can be moments of redefinition and renewed energy.

Using the coping steps identified above, how well are you navigating transitions?

Chapter 14
IN PURSUIT OF LEGACY

"The legacy you leave is the life you lead."

—JIM KOUZES AND BARRY POSNER

If I asked you, "What is your legacy?" would you have an answer?

Most people don't know what their legacy is. They have an idea of what they're good at and what they want from their career, but they have no solid answer as to how they can actually make a lasting impact.

Merriam-Webster's 11th Collegiate Dictionary defines "legacy" as 1) "A gift by will especially of money or other personal property" and 2) "Something transmitted by or received from an ancestor or predecessor or from the past"; <the *legacy* of ancient philosophers>

However, a legacy goes beyond a will or ancestry. It is something that anyone, no matter their age, leadership experience, or station in life, can and should put into place. I've chosen to redefine "legacy" for myself as "a selfless act requiring one to pursue a sustainable impact on the next generations or group of leaders." When we live our daily lives demonstrating how we make the world we inhabit a better place, then we have found it!

Without legacy, you risk living a life subjected to responding to what's happening around you instead of an intentional journey that defines you and propels you to move forward. Having clarity about your legacy no matter where you are as a leader is essential to understanding who you are and the real difference you can make. Legacy is something you create through your everyday actions and choices.

Here are three ways to fully embrace your life's legacy and make your mark of significance.

1. Legacy is selfless, not self-promoting.
2. Legacy is a desire to leave things better than before.
3. Legacy has a sustainable and lasting impact.

Let's explore these three points.

1. Legacy is selfless, not self-promoting.

   Legacy requires you to shift your mind-set from desiring success to achieving significance. When you think about your career, do you think of it as a job—a paycheck? Or is it a platform for you to leverage and make a meaningful difference? I spent most of my career wanting to be successful—measuring my worth against traditional metrics such as salary, promotions, and recognition by my supervisors. And while striving to achieve the next level of leadership is admirable, it is simply an aspiration—not a legacy. Instead of focusing on the next career opportunity, focus on the impact you are making on others.

2. Legacy is a desire to leave things better than before.

   It's important to look for ways to turn your accomplishments into an opportunity for someone else. No matter your role, you have a responsibility to pave the way for the person or team behind you. Teach them how to achieve what they want by not sacrificing who they are.

   As a senior executive at Walmart, my legacy for the Women's Officer Caucus was to lift them up, to help them find their voice, and to make their time at Walmart one of significance, knowing their value, empowered to make a meaningful difference, encouraged and surrounded by a sisterhood of support. I am confident my impact had a ripple effect beyond the Women's Officer Caucus.

3. Legacy has a sustainable and lasting impact.

Part of defining and living out your legacy every day starts with knowing your foundational values in all areas of life. In other words, you don't leave one part of your life and turn to focus on your legacy, which all of a sudden becomes clear. You must take the different elements of your life—such as spirituality, family, career, and fitness—blend them together, and make them an authentic part of who you are every day. When you do this, others notice and will do the same—resulting in a domino effect across the different circles of your life.

Why is leaving a legacy important?

Sometimes we define who we are on the basis of our job or how successful we are in our careers. We define who we are by our children and our worth as their guardians. This was a trap I fell into—defining myself and my purpose by my job and my success at Walmart. Legacy is different than achievement. Beyond your family and your responsibilities, it is your specific calling. Your legacy is rooted in your identity.

Is your inner voice a barrier or a powerful ignition to your legacy?

Do you use powerful, uplifting words when leading others and then flip into a negative choice of words when your inner voice speaks? I still fight this struggle today. I have found the power of lifting others up and putting wind beneath their wings. And in the next breath, I hear critical and demeaning words inside my head, causing me self-doubt and feelings of inferiority. This may surprise you, considering that I've been a seasoned executive with one of the largest companies in the world. But we are all human! Humans are often faced with self-doubt, blind spots, or limiting beliefs.

Changing the tone and words in your self-talk is an important daily practice that can be mastered, and mastering positive self-talk is critically important for us to see what is possible so that we are not limited by barriers of poor personal perception.

When I see that behavior in others, I call them out to stop and recalibrate. When I see that behavior in myself, I say, "Tell that bitch inside my head to shut up!" (It works for me!)

Words are powerful and can change lives.

Tammy Kling, my coauthor and the CEO of OnFire Books Leadership Company, has built her brand on teaching leaders that *Words are Currency*. She is a world changer with the gift to change lives through words. Here is one practical application of a lesson I learned from her. What are the words you want to eliminate from your inner-voice vocabulary? What are the positive and powerful words you want to replace them with? Write them down and build a daily practice of mastering positive self-talk.

The Importance of a Personal Mission Statement

If you don't invest the time to find your purpose and live up to it, you may wander and flounder. Or, worse yet, you may let someone else define your purpose and mission for you!

Your personal mission statement will grow and evolve throughout your life. It will be tested and challenged. But make the personal commitment to invest in it. It will require personal discovery, with the goal to be living with a sense of destiny, passion, and excitement.

I recently took a leadership assessment survey, and March to a Mission was one of the principles they were measuring. It was described in the following way: "the tendency to live

with and make choices supporting a sense of purpose in life."
My score was a ten out of ten. A sense of purpose has been
an important part of my life.

Here is a model I have used to help myself and others
develop a powerful personal mission statement.

Step 1: Start with understanding your Why.

Simon Sinek, author of *Start With Why: How Great Leaders
Inspire Everyone to Take Action*, has a great model for getting
past your What and your How to discover your Why. He
calls it "The Golden Circles—What/How/Why." Sinek
writes, "Inspired Leaders think, act, and communicate from
the inside out. People don't buy what you do; they buy
why you do it." Using this metaphor, people are choosing
every day to "buy" a relationship with you—or not. You
are a brand. To be a person of influence, you need people
"buying" your brand.

What is your Why? Having a personal mission statement
brings focus and purpose to your life. Here are some real-life
examples:

Oprah Winfrey, Founder of OWN, The Oprah Winfrey
Network: "To be a teacher. And to be known for inspiring
my students to be more than they thought they could be."

Eric Schmidt, CEO, Google: "My mission is to collect all
of the world's information and make it accessible to everyone."

Sam Walton, founder of Walmart Inc.: "To work together,
to lower the cost of living for everyone, giving the world an
opportunity to see what it's like to save and have a better life."

Step 2: Start by choosing your values.

Values are a personal choice you make about what's
important to you. Being guided by your highest values

brings immense satisfaction and meaning. Examples of lifetime values are the seven Fs:

Family, Firm (or career), Fitness (physical or mental), Faith, Friendship, Finance, Fun. (From the book *Achieving Authentic Success* by Dr. Ron Jensen)

Choose your top three. It may be hard to narrow your top to just three. But focus allows you to dig deep into your priorities.

ACTION: Write down your top three values as the start to your personal mission statement.

Step 3: Choose your mission.

An essential next step is to write down your personal mission statement. Craft your mission statement, and continue to refine it. It will likely take many drafts to get it just right.

Ask yourself, "What is my calling, my life's aim? What inspires me the most? What activity or service are my core values urging me to pursue? What makes me great?"

This step takes introspection and selecting just the right words to express your mission. Invest the time to become a wordsmith.

Step 4: Put it all together.

A template I found that helps me link the three elements above is as follows:

The value you create + who you're creating it for + the expected outcome.

Your life is worth a noble mission!

Take action by writing your statement down, being sure you have linked all three components.

Then share it with others whom you trust, and ask for their feedback.

And try it on for size. Declare it with those who matter most to you. Evaluate your daily actions to see if they align with your mission statement. Is it authentic to you? Is it noble, and does it fill you with pride when done well?

My Personal Mission Statement:

My life's mission is to use my voice for women and children and break through barriers that limit their ability to be significant.

On the basis of my statement, it makes sense that I am drawn to organizations focused on children's health, education, and women's empowerment. One organization that brings me joy in having established is the Women's Officer Caucus at Walmart Inc. Every female officer (VP, SVP, EVP and president) of the company is a member. The purpose of the group is to attract and retain our officers, to create a network for support and accountability, to mentor and invest in high-potential future officers, and to give back to the community.

We hear often from the women officers how welcomed and supported they feel working inside the company. The greatest compliment I heard about the WOC came from a fellow male SVP who recognized our group for the camaraderie and incredible sense of belonging and support that the women in our officer ranks find so reinforcing. Other leadership groups are trying to find their way to replicate the empowerment and support this resource group provides.

Learning to march to your mission will help you find your fit inside an organization. I have found that you will also discover your voice to share ideas and to confront challenges. It has been one of the most important tools I use to say yes to projects or nonprofit organizations with which I choose to volunteer my time and gifts. It has also given me clarity and permission to say no to requests that do not align with my mission statement.

Saying no when you are not aligned order to avoid feeling overcommitted or resentful, is a very powerful way to march to your mission. Saying no is often a hard thing to do, especially when you cannot also share why you've said no. But you don't have to have a reason. This is where most people go astray in their life activities and get overscheduled. They feel as if they've got to have a reason to say no. Sometimes the answer is just no, for no reason at all. If you feel as if you've got to come up with a reason for not getting overcommitted, get clarity on your goals. Say no to anything that detracts from your goals.

Saying that this is not a place or cause that seems to fit or align with my mission statement is much more respectful than just saying no. You may have to explain what exactly you mean by what does align, but you will have to find the right words to be articulate and caring.

The goal of this chapter is to inspire you to find more meaning in all that you do. Don't wait until later in life to make your mark. Instead, fully embrace the power of your legacy and what it can mean for your life today. When you do, you'll notice that success alone is far less important—and that significance will truly change your impact. I know I aim to be in the 2-percent category of those who know their legacy and live it. For me, that means a life of mentorship and servant leadership. If I can help just one leader find their way and encourage them to live up to their fullest potential, I've made a difference.

What about you?

Legacy

What is Your Legacy?

1. Commit it to paper.

2. Evaluate the words in your legacy statement. Are they positive and powerful? Have you mastered the power of positive and empowering self-talk?

3. Put your legacy statement to the test. Are your spending time investing in bringing your legacy to life? If the answer is no, it may be time to stop and to reevaluate how you are investing your time.

4. Establish ways to have a meaningful influence on those around you, starting today! One way to get started is by becoming a mentor. Mentorship is a hallmark of great leaders.

It's okay if you're not sure what your legacy is. But it's time to begin thinking about the ways you can impact others in the world and at work.

Chapter 15

INTEGRITY AND ETHICS

"Goodness is about character- integrity, honesty, kindness, generosity, moral courage, and the like. More than anything else, it is about how we treat people."

—DENNIS PRAGER

From Hollywood scandals to business failures of enormous magnitude, it's evident that we are living in the midst of an integrity crisis. As we read and hear about these issues, we can see that lines have been undoubtedly crossed. This is not a political statement, but a fact-based observation about what's at the core of decision making.

Still, how do we lead when ethical lines are vague and, at best, gray?

As a parent or someone in leadership, you will inevitably make choices within gray areas rather than those in black-and-white. Let's start with establishing a definition of integrity. Part of the problem today is that people have different definitions of integrity and, therefore, different and varied thresholds of measurement.

The definition I like best is, "Integrity is a concept of consistency of actions, values, methods, measures, principles, expectations, and outcomes. In ethics, integrity is regarded as the honesty and truthfulness or accuracy of one's actions." Integrity means doing the right thing at all times and in all circumstances, even when no one is looking. Critical components of these definitions are consistency, actions, measures, honesty, and truthfulness. These can all be observed and taught through consistency of actions and behaviors. When you see or work with persons of high integrity, their integrity shows at work and in their personal lives. It is inspiring to work for a company and leaders who teach and celebrate integrity and ethics consistently and often. It is not a word on the wall of values; it is alive and held as a standard for all. At the core are decision-making and behavioral choices. When faced with a gray-area scenario, you must face into it, examine the facts, and execute your decision with integrity.

A personal story about integrity happened when I was leading membership at Sam's Club. I had traveled to

Louisville, Kentucky, with Kenny Folk, the regional vice president and a true mentor to me and so many others in the club business. I learned so much from Kenny, such as his question, "Who's that member?" And I learned from him how to inspire a team to perform beyond their wildest dreams. On this trip, we were visiting a club that was getting the gift of a brand new facility—relocating their current club. But their membership base needed to dramatically increase to ensure they had the traffic and the strong business member base to be profitable. Charlie Waggoner was the market manager. We attended the club's morning meeting, and I was shocked to see that Charlie had shaved his head! What would make him do something so drastic? He had challenged the associates in that club to raise more money this year than last year for their children's hospital. If they did, he would shave his head. We were there for the big revelation. He had shaved his head! I was the next person to speak at the morning meeting, and I had an important membership goal challenge to share with them. Their membership drives had been slow, and they needed to step up the results. I challenged them to double their membership sales before the Grand Opening, and I said that if they did, I would shave my head!

Well, they did that, and more! I was amazed and afraid. I had made a commitment. And now I had to deliver. But I was a girl. Not one of the leaders was going to hold me to my word.

But I had to be true to my word, especially because I was a woman. At the Fall Managers Meeting, while on stage, I challenged the leaders to shave my head. They could not do it; they were truly going to give me a pass. Even Kenny Folk, who was as courageous as they come, had no intention of shaving my head. He eventually cut off a few very short pieces of hair. But the stylist on stage had to finish the job by

cutting my hair to one-half inch and colored what was left
half blue and half green (the Sam's Club colors). To this day,
I still wear short hair because of that challenge. The bonus? I
earned the respect of all those managers because I lived up to
my word.

In any leadership role, whether it be CEO, chief financial
officer, entrepreneur, or leader of teams, you must find
the courage to make the tough choices, even in the gray.
Here are five ways to avoid an integrity crisis and actively
eliminate the gray lines of leadership.

1. **Know your core values.** When you face a situation
   that completely throws you off, start with having
   a clear understanding of the personal values you
   hold dear. Take a step back and look at the situation
   with a neutral perspective. What will you stand for?
   What are the things that deeply motivate you and
   inspire you to do your best work? What are your
   nonnegotiables? Taking time to evaluate and define
   your central core values and beliefs will position you
   for success as you navigate unexpected left turns.

2. **Is it legal? Is it wise?** One of the principles I was
   taught early in my career is to ask two questions: "Is
   it legal?" and, "Is it wise?" Those are two different
   questions, but they both must be answered. Applying
   that lens to everyday behavior is essential for leading
   as a high-integrity individual. You can always use
   probing questions such as, "Why do you want to get
   into that?" "Why do you want to cross that line?" "Is
   there anything that is going to be better because you
   crossed it?" These questions will help your process
   your decision making in every situation.

3. **Take swift action.** When it comes down to making
   the tough calls, it's important not to hesitate, no

matter how difficult the decision. Time does not make the situation better or easier. I learned this the hard way by letting bad performance or poor decision making linger in the hopes that I could influence my team members' behavior through private conversations and placing them in different situations. It was my attempt at rehabilitation. However, one of the critical lessons I learned was to discern the difference between an integrity issue and a lack of skill for the job. The quicker you can take action when faced with an integrity issue, the clearer you can set the standard for other team members.

4. **Treat people with fairness and dignity.** Whether in the small actions you take or the large decisions you make, showing care and concern for the people you lead can be a defining moment for earning their trust and respect. Mike Duke, former CEO of Walmart Inc. was the gold-standard leader for integrity and respect. He had very high standards of performance that he would communicate clearly and often. But when he had to make a tough call to let someone go, he was swift, decisive, and respectful. I remember a time when Mike had to let one of the leadership team members go for a violation of company policy. He kept the details of the situation very private to protect the dignity of the leader, but he called each one of us who worked on the leadership team to advise us of his decision. He did not want us to hear it secondhand, and he wanted us to be informed when our people asked questions the next day. The role of great leaders is to create a place where your team can work with dignity and respect, then to reward them with an environment where they can flourish. That is when you change as

a leader—from someone who wants to be the best in his or her role to someone who wants to see everyone perform at their best. Not only will your life change as a leader, but the lives of everyone you interact with will change, as well.

5. **Be transparent.** If you make a mistake you need to own it, even if it's tough to swallow. When I have made an honest mistake, it was always best for me to own it and bring it to the attention of my supervisor so that we could find a solution in the full light of others who I would enlist to correct the situation. Admitting a mistake is very hard for the ego of many executives. And here is the root of many a failed leader. Being humble and asking for help are always better than covering up a mistake and running the risk of compounding the issue. Learn from your mistakes, and do not repeat them. The respect you earn by being open and transparent is one that builds your reputation of trust and integrity. In addition, it makes you more human and approachable.

Another important reason for transparency is that, during times of change and uncertainty, associates want to be a part of a culture that puts a premium on telling the truth. When we were leading store operations through changes in structure and streamlined operating procedures, we wanted to be the ones to share the news with our associates, including the impact it would have on them. We strived to be the leaders who shared the news first with truth and genuine care for our people.

There is a reason why practicing integrity is not always easy. But when we choose to make the right decisions, even in the grittiest moments, we will reap the rewards that come from making the right calls. I am proud to have worked for a company that teaches, celebrates, reinforces, and holds itself to the highest standards of integrity. Integrity is the foundation of the culture at Walmart. We are taught that integrity is not just a corporate responsibility but a personal one as well.

Integrity and Ethics

What is your definition of integrity?

- Are your behavioral expectations clear and never compromised?

- Do you make it a point to teach, celebrate, and hold each other to the highest standards of integrity?

- Do you have a relationship of trust built between you and the people you lead?

These questions are designed to make you think.

It's never too late to evaluate yourself and your own behavior and make a course correction. Consider a life and career rooted in uncompromising integrity. It's a fundamental pillar of great leaders, and it will rub off on everyone around you.

Chapter 16
SO WHAT?

"If we are to achieve a richer culture, rich in contrasting values, we must recognize the whole gamut of human potentialities, and so we weave a less arbitrary social fabric, one in which each diverse human gift will find a fitting place."

—MARGARET MEAD

So now that I have shared my story, so what? How can you apply it to your own life?

Throughout these personal stories and leadership moments of putting ourselves out there and encouraging more women and diverse talent to be seated at the table, you might think we have made great strides. What are the results of all our efforts and sacrifices? We may have made progress in a lot of areas, but there's still room for improvement. Let's look at the facts.

Despite all the talk and acknowledgement by boards of directors and shareholders, the latest data shows minimal representation of women in board seats (17 percent at the top fifty companies★) and even lower numbers in executive-committee positions (12 percent★). Gender equality in the corporate world is now an unavoidable topic for boards and shareholders. (★Source: McKinsey & Company study results, 10/6/17.)

Numerous studies from McKinsey, Catalyst.org, the World Economic Forum, and others have documented the performance advantages of gender and ethnic diversity, including higher returns on investment, increased profitability, and a greater ability to attract and retain talent.★ (★Source: Network of Executive Women research, Winning with Women on Purpose, 2017.) Yet women make up half of the world's working-age population but generate only 37 percent of the GDP.

Companies are filled with talented women! Female college graduates have outnumbered males for decades, and recent research from Catalyst.org revealed that women made up nearly half of the labor force (44 percent). However, representation drops at every progressive level of leadership to 35 percent of midlevel managers, 25 percent of executives, and only 5 percent of CEOs.★ (★Source: Fortune. com/2017/09/28/women-c-suite-CEOs.)

These statistics should alarm us all—not just women, but all stakeholders and senior leaders. How do we make real, sustainable improvements? The answer I see lies in working together to make intentional progress. We must understand what is getting in the way of women winning at higher levels and what motivates them to stay in the game. This is not just a women's issue. It requires the work of men and women together.

So how do we break the cycle? A recent Network of Executive Women (NEW) research white paper found four big ideas that have merit for working together to address breaking the cycle.

1. Rethink how we identify potential.

2. Focus on career sponsorship.

3. Increase the representation of women and diverse talent in "feeder" positions for senior executive roles and potential board roles.

4. CEO involvement and transformational inclusion and "unconscious bias" programs driven from the top, along with persistence and management commitment.

Let's understand the expectations for each of these actions.

Rethink how we identify potential: One contributing factor is that men are promoted on the basis of potential and that women are promoted on the basis of delivered results, as captured in studies by McKinsey and by Catalyst.org and in Sheryl Sandberg's research in her book, *Lean In: Women, Work, and the Will to Lead*. Therefore, women and men should be assigned stretch assignments at equal rates.

Next, we must find a more objective way to identify potential. It cannot be an instinct or a judgement call. It needs to be based on observable behaviors that can predict potential. We used leadership competencies at Walmart in our talent review, talent development, and performance evaluation processes. Competencies such as intellectual curiosity, drive for results, synthesizing strategic choices, managing diverse relationships, building talent pipelines, innovation management, and strategic and organizational agility were critical priorities based upon the growth and critical skills required to lead in a dynamic marketplace.

And last in this category, we must build talent pipelines and succession plans that have equal representation of high-potential women and men.

Focus on career sponsorship

Much of my career was focused on identifying and providing mentors for up-and-coming talent. This was certainly a helpful development initiative. But the critical need is for key leaders to sponsor equal numbers of women and men.

A sponsor is very different from a mentor. A mentor provides advice and support, but a sponsor uses his or her organizational influence to advocate for individuals when making stretch-assignment decisions and promotion decisions. Sponsor relationships take time to develop; sponsorship comes to those the leader knows well. And high-potential talent should work to build sponsor relationships with both men and women. What does this mean in your own life? It means fighting for yourself by being a leader that is both gracious and strong, as well as competent. It means being your own advocate inside the organization.

In my own career, a breakthrough moment occurred when I was promoted from vice president to senior vice president. I had been recruited and hired by an exceptional woman, Suzanne Alford, who had asked me to join the Sam's Club organization after observing me serve as a leader during the PACE acquisition. I had the privilege to learn from and work with her for three years. When she made the personal decision to leave Sam's Club and relocate to San Antonio, Texas, she submitted my name as her replacement. I went through all the leadership approvals and was offered the role of SVP, responsible for all the support functions at Sam's Club. Suzanne was my sponsor. I may never have been considered for the role without her advocacy and support.

When you read this, hopefully it will make you think of the key authentic relationships you should build in order to help you reach your goals. Relationships are the key to success in life—not only in your business but in every area. Think of ways that you can build them authentically, but be intentional about contacting key people who can sponsor you along the way. Don't be timid about setting your intentions and goals.

Item number three on the list is to increase the representation of women and diverse talent in "feeder" positions for senior-executive roles and board "feeder" positions. This is all about building diverse talent-succession pipelines for the most critical positions identified in your organizations.

We called them the Top Fifty Critical Roles, and we reviewed the talent identified for these positions at least twice a year. We also developed individualized development plans for leaders in the pipeline to ensure readiness for promotion when positions were open. Ensuring a diverse pipeline is required to achieve talent readiness when opportunities become available.

Providing women and diverse talent experience in P&L (profit and loss) roles is a critical component to preparing them for senior-executive positions. One of the best pieces of advice I ever received was from David Glass, when I was offered a P&L role at Sam's Club. I was on a career track to succeed the chief human resources (we called it people) executive. When presented with the opportunity to lead a large P&L, Mr. Glass's advice was, "Go for it! You can always get back into the People Division later in your career." I have shared this sage advice with so many high-potential individuals. It will be hard to get to the top of your organization if you have not demonstrated success when leading a P&L. Take the opportunity when it is presented!

The final idea from the white paper is CEO involvement. That means establishing transformational inclusion and "unconscious bias" programs. Those programs must be driven from the top, along with persistence and management commitment.

This is critical.

I cannot stress the importance of CEO involvement. It is all about tone at the top. When the CEO identifies inclusion and diversity as a top priority, they get implemented. The key differentiator is the CEO holding their direct reports and all management levels accountable for their behaviors and results. This requires adherence by inspecting talent pipelines and talent promotions and by identifying the critical behaviors expected from the senior leaders. When ongoing adherence occurs, a company can move from implementation to true culture integration.

All of these actions can be distilled down to the following:

- Placing women in big jobs.
- Supporting women.
- Recognizing and dismantling unconscious bias.

I must give credit for these three fundamental ideas to research done by NEW (Network of Executive Women). Their research and practical ideas for changing the trajectory of gender equality are practical, tactical, and game changing. If you are not familiar with NEW, please connect with them at newonline.org. I find their conclusions in this research to be on the mark!

The solutions will not be found by men alone. The solutions will not be found by women alone. The solutions must be identified and implemented together! This is not an optics problem. This will require systemic change and courageous leadership from all of us who care to change the game.

To all leaders, I encourage you to be intentional when developing women and people of color. Promote potential that is equally measured on the competencies required for personal and business success.

Seek to understand the challenges of leaders who are not like you. Pause to be sure you are considering all talent equally. Inclusion requires listening, and ensuring that every voice is heard. Stop and ask for all people to share their points of view before making the final decision. Ask to hear from all people seated at the table, especially those who have not spoken up.

Women, we have a responsibility to be authentic leaders and come prepared to be excellent. **(Authentic Leadership)**

Choose to make the hard-right decision to fall forward in the face of adversity. **(Falling Forward)**

Expand your networks, and do not keep yourself in isolation. **(Leadership Is about Relationships)**

Change the voice in your head to one of confidence and belief in yourself. **(In Pursuit of Legacy)**

Navigate successfully through the challenges of life and leadership. **(Unexpected Left Turns)**

Inspire others to be a part of your journey; then make it worthwhile for them. **(Be a Visionary)**

When given the opportunity to use your voice, understand that it is your responsibility to own it. **(Define Your Bright Lines)**

Align yourself with people and organizations that possess your values. **(Culture Is the Great Differentiator)**

Take thoughtful risks that are right for you and your family. **(Fears and Limiting Belief)**

Be a great mentor, as well as a great sponsor. **(Be Known)**

Demonstrate excellence in the What and the How. **(The Secret Ingredient: Resilience)**

Leave things better than before by leaving a lasting imprint. **(Making an Impact)**

Pull other women and men up with you along the way. **(My life's journey in *Gracious and Strong*)**

This is a matter of crisis. We must find the way to make sustainable progress.

You have to lead differently. You are the key to change for women and diverse leadership. You have to take responsibility for your preparedness and take up where my generation left off. It's important to note here that my generation made the case for change by making the business case for equality. And we did make the case. But sustainable change will require winning much more than the intellectual case for change. This we have proven. We have inspired a dream that visionary men and courageous women will deliver.

You

What does all of this mean for you?

It means that in your own career you can be bold and visionary. Don't accept the current state of reality and make it acceptable. You can be the spark who makes the difference, who stands up and says, "I will not sit idly by while we take steps backwards from the incredible progress made towards women and diverse leaders being prepared to grow and promote and create change."

Do you accept this truly personal challenge?

Will you be the spark for change?

Can you inspire action that will deliver sustainable progress?

Of course, you can.

The future is in your hands!

SOURCES

Age Wave, Ameriprise Financial and Harris Interactive; based on The New Retirement Mindscape Study[SM], 2005.

Why Are Women Still Set Up to Fail in the C-Suite? By Cynthia Soledad, September 28, 2017, Fortune.com

IMA Worldwide, Reaction Pattern to Negative Change; Reaction Pattern to Positive Change. "©IMA. Confidential. Adapted with Permission. www.imaworldwide.com"

An Acceleration is Needed to Ensure Gender Equality, by Eric Labaye, Senior Partner (Director) at McKinsey & Company, Chairman McKinsey Global Institute, 10/6/17. Featured in: Professional Women.

Network of Executive Women research, Winning with Women: On Purpose, March 29, 2017.

As I was writing this book, Walmart underwent a corporate name change from Wal-Mart Stores, Inc., to Walmart Inc. Throughout the book when I'm addressing the Walmart enterprise (Walmart U.S., Sam's Club, International and E-Commerce operations) I used its new corporate name of Walmart Inc.

IMA Reaction Patterns to Change Models

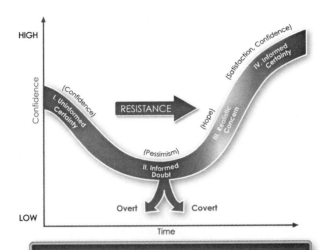

Reaction Pattern to a Positive Change: Levels of confidence in successful implementation.

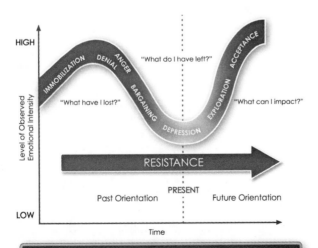

Reaction Pattern to a Negative Change: Is caused more by the loss of control than the content of the change.

culture champion
women's empowerment
Resilient humility
SMART brave INVESTOR
composed ENERGY Walmart AMAZING champion LOYAL authentic
tenacious FRIEND concise honest Enthusiastic LEADER
Respectful Kind dynamic INTEGRITY BOLD AMBASSADOR
authentic mentor FOCUSED courageous calm empowering PIONEER
INDEPENDENT vivacious JOYFUL GIVING innovator
generous SPARK paving the path for women advocate inclusive Brilliant
FRIEND trusted INTELLIGENT articulate motivating relationship expert legacy
Confidence GIFTED stalwart SERVANT trailblazer
awesome role model compassionate
kind Professional success extraordinary FRIEND
INSIGHTFUL Resilient
laugh
AWESOME
Comm
war

Celia Swanson

There aren't enough words to express our appreciation. Thank you from the WOC.

Walmart ✳